introductory
Financial Economics
with Spreadsheets

introductory
Financial Economics
with Spreadsheets

Cornelis van de Panne
Department of Economics
University of Calgary
Canada

 harwood academic publishers
Australia • Canada • China • France • Germany • India • Japan
Luxembourg • Malaysia • The Netherlands • Russia • Singapore • Switzerland

Copyright © 1999 OPA (Overseas Publishers Association) N.V. Published by license under the
Harwood Academic Publishers imprint, part of The Gordon and Breach Publishing Group.

Amsteldijk 166
1st Floor
1079 LH Amsterdam
The Netherlands

British Library Cataloguing in Publication Data

A catalogue record for this book is available from the British Library.

ISBN 90-5702-364-4

Contents

part 1 Spreadsheets and Budgets

part 2 Basic Concepts of Financial Economics

part 3 Project Evaluation

part 4 Database Management Applications

Preface

For more than a decade, spreadsheets have been the principal tool for performing tasks related to management, administration, and economics. Spreadsheet commands and functions have been designed with these tasks in mind.

Manuals and books explaining spreadsheets concentrate on computational details without any background in finance or economics, on which the corresponding spreadsheets features are based. On the other hand, there exist a large number of books dealing with finance and economics, which have been written under the assumption that the reader will have at most a calculator available for calculations.

This book links both approaches, and demonstrates and explains both spreadsheet features and financial economics background by presenting a large variety of basic applications in business and economics. It integrates the spreadsheet tool in the explanation of the material, so that the reader becomes familiar with both.

The book is, in the first place, intended for persons who are using the basic features of the Microsoft® Excel spreadsheet but wish to extend their use of the spreadsheet for a variety of business and personal applications. For example, engineers who have some management functions may wish to use the concepts of engineering economics in terms of spreadsheets, and accountants who are familiar with economic evaluations, may wish to use the advanced spreadsheets tools to enhance their analysis. But also persons without much of a background in business or economics, who are using spreadsheets can utilize the book to obtain an understanding of and a capability to work with spreadsheet functions and commands related to business and economics.

Secondly, the material can be used in courses in business and economics. The sixteen chapters, divided into four parts, provide ample material for at least one course. Some chapters may also be used as supplements for certain other courses. The notes on which the book is based were originally developed for a course on computer applications in economics.

To Johanna

Acknowledgements

As the material on which the book is based has been used over one and a half decades in courses, my indebtedness has grown in proportion. The idea that basic financial economics is an important subject can be traced back to the engineers Job and Michiel, who commented that engineering economics, that stepchild of the economics teaching program, is the most useful course in economics.

Many hundreds of students, both undergraduate and graduate, have been subjected to less perfect versions of the material and have sweated on the assignments in the form of gruelling three-hour computer-based exams, enabling me to spot shortcomings and deficiencies. They also have encouraged me by their appreciation of the material, convincing me that the approach taken was worthwhile.

I have been encouraged at various times by colleagues who reviewed the work, namely Norman Cameron, University of Manitoba, Peter Bell, University of Western Ontario, and Les Woods, Lincoln University. I also benefited from a special one semester teaching relief awarded to me by the University of Calgary to complete the manuscript. Mr Jacob Piera helped to debug and enhance the material. My wife Johanna caught a number of imperfections in the proofs.

part 1

Spreadsheets and Budgets

Chapter 1
Spreadsheet Background and Basics

This chapter introduces the fundamentals of spreadsheets and Microsoft®Excel. Advantages of spreadsheets in general are discussed and some historical details are given. Entering text, numbers and formulas are indicated, as well as saving and opening of spreadsheet files.

In this chapter you will learn the following spreadsheet commands, features, and functions:

- Formulas
- Sum
- Formula display
- Save, Save as
- Exit, Quit
- Open

1.1 The Essence of Spreadsheets

A computer spreadsheet is a tool for working with numbers.

Numbers must be accompanied by verbal descriptions to make sense of them and to provide context. Consider the example of a travel expenses claim, see Panel 1.1, which represents handwriting on a sheet of paper.

Panel 1.1 Travel Expenses Claim

Travel Expense Claim		
Airline Ticket	$	478.34
Hotel Bill	$	258.73
Shuttle	$	16.00
Parking	$	14.50
Meals	$	80.75
Total Expenses	$	848.32

Each item consists of two parts: (1) a *description* of the item, (2) its *amount*. For example, the first item may be described as Airline Ticket, and its amount at $478.34. The following four items are similar. The amount of Total Expenses is the sum of the five numbers above it, which is obtained by the addition of these numbers, either 'manually' or by some calculator.

A tool for working with numbers, such as a spreadsheet, must therefore be able to work with the text of descriptions and work with numbers. It must therefore have both *word processing* capabilities and *calculating* capacities.

When work is done on a sheet of paper, descriptions and amounts are put in specific places along horizontal and vertical lines, sometimes printed on the paper such as the horizontal lines in Panel 1.1, or left to the imagination, as in the case of the vertical lines. The arrangement on the page makes it easier to understand what is represented. A spreadsheet has the same organization in terms of horizontal and vertical lines, or rows and columns. The name *spreadsheet*, which has its origin in accounting, refers to this organization in rows and columns.

A spreadsheet can be characterized as a combination of a word processor and a calculator operating in an environment organized in rows and columns.

The computer spreadsheet can be considered as an extension of the sheet of paper. Its two main advantages over sheets of paper are:

1. It can perform arithmetical and other operations on the amounts of the items.
2. Whereas what is written on paper is difficult to change (by erasing and rewriting), parts of computer spreadsheets are changed easily.

These two advantages are mutually enhancing because after a value has been changed calculations can be redone effortlessly and usually automatically. The computer spreadsheet can be seen as the natural extension and the natural successor of the lined paper sheet with columns. This explains the widespread adoption of spreadsheets and the commercial success of companies producing the software.

Many other features have been added to spreadsheets, such as graphing, data processing, and programming capabilities, but their inclusion has been a consequence of the success of the basic concept of a spreadsheet as a combination of a word processor and a calculator working in a grid environment.

1.2 The Background of Spreadsheets

The idea of computer spreadsheets originated with Dan Bricklin who developed one in 1978 while working on his MBA at the Harvard Business School. In 1979 he introduced, together with Don Fylstra and Bob Franklin, a commercial version called VisiCalc (Visible Calculator) for the Apple II microcomputer. This program became quite successful with business. Spreadsheet use by corporations became almost universal after the IBM-PC microcomputer was launched in 1981, and Mitch Kapor introduced his spreadsheet Lotus 1-2-3 in 1982. Lotus was larger and faster than VisiCalc and had a very effective command structure. Moreover, it contained, in addition to the spreadsheet, graphics and database facilities.

Today, many other spreadsheets exist, such as Microsoft® Excel, Quattro and

Wingz, and spreadsheets are included in integrated packages such as Microsoft® Office®. Spreadsheets of different software companies are fiercely competitive, so that the features of comparable versions are about the same. They may be different in terms of commands and tools, but in almost all cases equivalents can be found. Details of display may be different, but these are relatively unimportant. There may be certain advanced features unique to a spreadsheet, but all basic and standard tools are present in all spreadsheets. File formats are different, but files can be converted into common formats. A person proficient in the use of one spreadsheet will have no difficulty with using others.

In this book the Excel spreadsheet is used, because it is widely available and installed on many computers. Excel 97 for Microsoft® Windows® (Microsoft® Excel 98 for Macintosh) is employed, though this is not essential, as earlier versions or later ones differ only in less important details.

1.3 The Spreadsheet at Startup

The spreadsheet application or system, in this case Excel, is activated by selecting the package's icon, after which a blank worksheet appears, see Panel 1.2. The top row displays the *menubar*, which contains most of the spreadsheet commands. The next two rows, only partially displayed in Panel 1.2, are toolbars filled with icons for tools, which are mostly simple commands. The fourth row, displaying in Panel 1.2 the active cell's name A1, is called the *formula bar*.

The remainder of the panel contains the spreadsheet itself, with its name, which is the default name for a new workbook Workbook1, shown below the formula bar. Spreadsheet basics are best learned by exploration and trial and error, while more advanced spreadsheet features should be systematically studied. For this reason we shall initially ignore the menubar and toolbars, and introduce gradually the commands and tools that are needed at a certain point.

A worksheet consists of a number of columns identified by letters (Columns A–F in Panel 1.2) and a number of rows identified by numbers (Rows 1–11 in Panel 1.2). Cells can therefore be indicated by column letter and row number (the *cell address*), so that the top left-hand cell is A1, and so on. The number of rows and columns that can be used is very large, and limitations are only relevant for large worksheets. The columns after column Z are called AA, AB, ...,AZ, BA, .., IV.

At any time, one cell is ready for entering new content or changing its existing content. This is called the *active cell*, it is designated by the *cell pointer* or cursor, its name is found on the left-hand side in the formula bar, and its content is displayed in the right-hand side of this panel.

In Panel 1.2, which gives the spreadsheet at startup, the active cell is A1. This is called the *home* of the cursor. The Control+Home key combination returns the cell pointer to cell A1. The active cell can be changed using the cell pointer via the mouse, or using the direction keys; Panel 1.3 details the most important keyboard shortcuts.

Panel 1.2 A Blank Worksheet

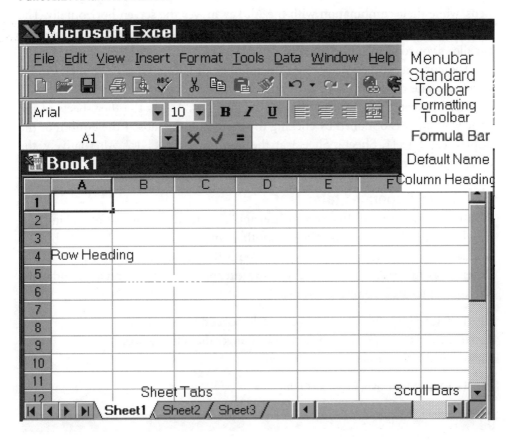

Panel 1.3 Keyboard Shortcuts for Movement

Key	Effect
←, ↑, ↓, →	One cell in indicated direction
Home	Moves to extreme left of row
Ctrl+Home	Moves to A1
Page Down	Down one screen
Page Up	Up one screen
Alt+Page Down	Right one screen
Alt+Page Up	Left one screen
Ctrl+Page Down	To next sheet in workbook
Ctrl+Page Up	To earlier sheet in workbook

The special Page-Up and Page-Down keys are used to navigate vertically in screen-size steps, while their combination with the Alt key moves the screen horizontally. The scroll bars on the right scroll the visible worksheet vertically, while the bottom scroll bar allows you to scroll it horizontally.

The current worksheet is one of a number of sheets which together form a *workbook*. The other sheets of a workbook may be used for related material with linkages between their information and calculations. Access to other sheets of the same workbook is obtained by clicking the mouse on the tabs at the bottom of the display, e.g. Sheet1, Sheet2, Sheet3 at the bottom of Panel 1.2. Alternatively, the Ctrl+Page Down or Up keyboard combination may be used, see Panel 1.3.

1.4 A Travel Expense Claim

We are now ready for our first spreadsheet application, which consists of making up a travel expense claim for a meeting in another city. The reader is advised to build a worksheet as indicated in the following. With the cursor at A1, we key in 'Travel Expense Claim', see Panel 1.4. As we type, the text appears in the formula bar and in the cell itself. Entering is completed by using:

1. the return key, after which the active cell moves downwards, or
2. an arrow key ($\leftarrow$, $\uparrow$, $\downarrow$, $\rightarrow$) which also changes the active cell, or
3. by clicking the mouse on another cell.

Panel 1.4 Sheet for Travel Expense Claim

	A	B	C	D	E
1	Travel Expense Claim				
2				Meals	
3	Airline Ticket	478.34			
4	Hotel Bill	258.73		Dinner 1	27
5	Shuttle	16		Breakfast 2	6.5
6	Parking	14.5		Dinner 2	40
7	Meals	80.75		Breakfast 3	7.25
8					
9	Total Expenses	848.32		Total Meals	80.75

Note that any text entered is automatically left-justified. The additional text is entered into cells A3 to A7 and A9 without difficulty. If, as in cell A1, the text is too large to be displayed in the cell, the space to the right is used, when the corresponding cell is empty. If not, the remaining part is not displayed (adjusting column widths is discussed later).

The numbers in cells B3 to B6 should be entered as digits, with a decimal point where needed. Numbers are displayed as right-justified. The system treats text and numbers quite differently, as many more things can be done with numbers than with text. If digits are mixed with letters, spaces, or other inappropriate keystrokes, the system considers the entry to be text and will left-justify the cell content. Should the display resulting from entering what is intended as a number be aligned to the left, an error must have been made.

The part of the worksheet dealing with meals is entered in columns D and E as shown in Panel 1.4. What is needed now are the totals for meals and for all expenses.

1.5 Formulas

Instead of numbers, a cell can contain a formula, which is an expression in terms of numbers and values of other cells. The spreadsheet system automatically executes any formula that appears in any of its cells and displays the resulting value. To indicate that the entry is a formula and not text it must start with an equal sign (=). The spreadsheet normally displays of a formula only its numerical value. The formula itself appears in the formula bar if the cell is the active cell.

The simplest formulas consist of numbers and arithmetical operations, such as 2.5+4. Panel 1.5 displays an enumeration of these operations and the symbols used in the spreadsheet, as well as an example.

Panel 1.5 Arithmetic Operations

Operation	Symbol	Example
Addition	+	=2+3
Subtraction	-	=3-1
Multiplication	*	=2*4
Division	/	=10/5
Exponentiation	^	=2^3

Parentheses may be employed to indicate the sequence of operations, for example (1+0.05)^6. Square and other roots can be written in terms of exponents.

In formulas we may use, instead of numbers, cell names, so that the content of the cell, which is presumed to be a value, is taken.

In the travel claim example presented in Panel 1.4 meals consists of a number of items, with descriptions in cells D4 to D7, and amounts in E4 to E7. The total amount for meals should be entered in E9. This is achieved by entering the following formula:

=E4+E5+E6+E7.

Note that a formula starts with the equal symbol (=). If it is not there, the system will consider the entry as text.

Instead of entering the cell names via the keyboard, the mouse or arrow keys may be used to move to the cell locations. The system then enters the corresponding cell name. If another operator or the return key or one of its its equivalents is keyed in, the pointer returns to the active cell. Entering cell names by pointing to the cells is usually more convenient and it may prevent typing errors.

We could also use the special built-in *function* SUM followed by the range of cells of which the sum should be taken:

=SUM(E4:E7).

A function consists of its *name*, here SUM (which may also be entered in lower case), and one or more *arguments* enclosed within parentheses. In this case the argument consist of the range of cells to be summed, indicated by the first and last cell name of the range, separated by a colon.

Another option is using the Microsoft® **AutoSum**™ tabulation tool represented by the button **S** of the standard toolbar. This tool automatically enters the sum function and a range of cells containing numbers above the active cell.

In our example, the number in cell E9 is used in B7 by entering in this cell the formula

=E9.

Total expenses of cell B9 are then generated by the formula

=SUM(B3:B7).

Normally, only the numbers resulting from formulas are displayed in cells, and the formulas are displayed in the formula bar only for the active cell. However, it is possible to display the formulas for all cells on the screen. This view of the spreadsheet is obtained by selecting from the **Tools** menu the **Preferences** item, after which the **View** menu appears (see Panel 1.6), of which the **Formulas** box is checked. For our example this results in the display in Panel 1.7.

1.6 File Operations

This completes building a simple worksheet for a travel expense claim. We may now wish to save it.

The worksheet is contained in a workbook with a number of empty sheets and this entire workbook must be saved (empty sheets, however, do not use up file space). A workbook can be saved with the **Save** or **Save As** command on the **File** menu.

The Save As command is used when the workbook has not been named (apart from its default name appearing on top of the sheet). In a computer lab environment the spreadsheet file for the workbook should normally be saved on the user's floppy disk. In other cases a specific directory on the hard drive will be preferred. In Excel for Windows the name supplied by the user will automatically be given the extension **.XLS**.

The Save command (keyboard shortcuts: **Ctrl+S** for Windows and **Cmd+S** for the Macintosh, also **Shift+F12**) is used to save over an existing file. The floppy disk button of the standard toolbar may also be employed.

Panel 1.6 The Preferences Menu

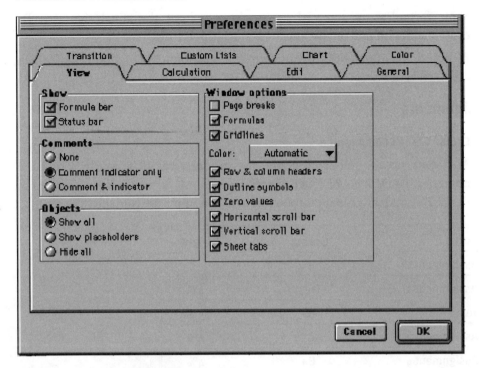

Panel 1.7 Formula View of Panel 1.4

	A	B	C	D	E
1	Travel Expense				
2				Meals	
3	Airline Ticket	478.34			
4	Hotel Bill	258.73		Dinner 1	27
5	Shuttle	16		Breakfast 2	6.5
6	Parking	14.5		Dinner 2	40
7	Meals	=E9		Breakfast 3	7.25
8					
9	Total Expenses	=SUM(B3:B8)		Total Meals	=SUM(E4:E8)

The **Save Workspace** command from the File menu refers to a set of workbooks that can be saved simultaneously. Such sets will not be used in this book.

To quit Excel, the **Exit** (Windows) (X from the keyboard may be entered when the menu is displayed) or **Quit** (Macintosh) command from the File menu is employed. A saved file is retrieved by selecting the **Open** command from the File menu.

This chapter and the remainder of this book deal only with the fundamental features of spreadsheets in general and Microsoft® Excel in particular, in as far as they are needed to obtain a working knowledge of spreadsheets for an introduction to financial economics. For more details consult the spreadsheet's manual and/or the **Help menu**.

Exercises

1.1 Some formulas are accepted as numbers without the equal sign (=). By experimentation find out for which formulas this is true.

1.2 By experimentation with the AutoSum™ tabulation tool (S), find out of which cells it takes the sum.

Assignments

1.1 Course Grade Point Average

A student has the following grades for various parts of a course. Using the numerical equivalents of letter grades, with A = 4, A- = 3.7, B+ = 3.3, B = 3, B- = 2.7,..., and the given percentage weight, determine the course letter grade.

Part	Grade	Weight
Assignment 1	B	4%
Assignment 2	A-	4%
Test 1	B+`	15%
Assignment 3	C	4%
Assignment 4	B+	4%
Test 2	A-	15%
Assignment 5	A	4%
Project	A-	20%
Final Examination	B+	30%

1.2. Annual Grade Point Average

Build a spreadsheet to calculate the grade point average for the year in which the following course grades were obtained. The numerical values of letter grades are as in Assignment 1.1.

AMAT211	B+	ECON301	A-
ECON311	A-	PHIL235	B+
BIOL201	B	FREN350	B+
ENGL340	C+	STAT218	A
STATS220	A	MAN350	B

1.3. Weekly Earnings of Part-time Job

Sally works part-time. For daytime work on a weekday she earns $7 per hour and for work at night $10 per hour. Create a spreadsheet for her weekly earnings. She worked the following hours: 4(D), 3(D), 5(N), 4(N), 0(D), 5(D), 3(D), where D = day and N = night.

References

Internet Sites:

This book:

www.acs.ucalgary.ca/~vandepan/inetcourse/finec/finec.html

Bricklin, Dan:

www.digitalcentury.com/encyclo/update/bricklin.html

www.nytsyn.com/live/Latest/149_052997_094208_7206.html

Spreadsheets:

Microsoft® Excel: www.microsoft.com/excel//Excel

Lotus: www.lotus.com/applicat/12397sp.htm/Lotus 123

Quattro Pro: www.corel.com/products/wordperfect/cqp7/index.htm/Quattro Pro

Printed Sources:

Microsoft® Corporation, *User's Guide Microsoft®Excel.*

Chapter 2
Simple Budgets with Spreadsheets

An example of a joint budget for two people sharing accommodation is used to demonstrate basic spreadsheet features and commands. Special attention is paid to worksheet appearance, editing, and copying.

In this chapter you will learn the following spreadsheet commands and functions:

- Change column width and row height
- Insert columns or rows
- Delete columns or rows
- Delete and clear
- Format numbers and text
- Move, copy, and paste
- Undo and redo
- Copy values
- Transpose ranges
- Relative and absolute cell references

2.1 A Simple Budget Worksheet

For almost everybody there are a number of tasks that involve calculations, such as devising budgets and filing tax returns. For the performance of these tasks, a calculator and pen and paper are usually sufficient, because the only operations involved are the four arithmetic ones to be found on a calculator. If some permanent account is required, titles and descriptions and the calculated numbers can be written down or entered in a word processor.

However, after a budget has been created for the first time, it usually happens that items have to be added or modified, so that most or all of the calculations must be redone. This may be repeated a number of times. The effort of making changes may prevent considering all possibilities, and can lead to a budget that does not reflect all expenditures or is inaccurate.

The use of a spreadsheet has the advantage that, once certain calculations have been set up, it is easy to make changes and additions. This will be demonstrated with a budget for two persons who have decided to live together in an apartment and share expenses. The data are as follows.

The apartment rent is $875 per month. Heating costs are estimated at $60 per month, power costs at $12 per month, and telephone rent at $14 per month. Groceries and meals are projected at $350 per month. As person A has more space available, it is agreed that this person will pay 60% of the space related costs, and person B 40%. Remaining costs are shared equally.

Panel 2.1 illustrates how a budget using these data would appear.

Panel 2.1 A Simple Joint Budget

Budget				
Space costs				
Apartment rent	$ 875			
Heating costs	$ 60			
Power	$ 12			
Total Space costs	$ 947			
Other costs				
Groceries, meals	$ 350			
Telephone rent	$ 14			
Total other costs	$ 364			
Space costs for A	60%	Space costs for B	40%	
Other costs for A	50%	Other costs for B	50%	
Costs for A		Costs for B		
Space costs	$ 568	Space costs	$ 379	
Other costs	$ 182	Other costs	$ 182	
Total	$ 750	Total	$ 561	

The two persons also wish to consider an apartment with a rent of $925, and subscribing to a newspaper and some magazines at $23 per month to be shared equally. Furthermore, they wish to reconsider the division of space costs, with A paying 57.5% instead of 60%. All of these changes may be examined separately as well as simultaneously. If a sheet of paper and a calculator are used, calculations must be redone for each of the many possible versions and the results rewritten on separate sheets of paper, while a spreadsheet only requires to enter the changes in the data to obtain immediately the desired results.

A spreadsheet version of the budget is set up as illustrated in Panel 2.2. The descriptions of the items are entered in column A and the amounts or values in column C. Note that the nonempty cells in columns A and C contain labels and those in columns C and G, values. For Total Space costs the formula =SUM(C4:C6) is entered in C7 using the AutoSum™ (S) tabulation tool, which results in a display of 947; for the total of Other costs the formula =SUM(C10:C11) is entered in C12, resulting in 364.

The space cost share of A of 60% or 0.6 is given explicitly in C14, and the space cost share of B is in G14 entered as =1–C14. In the same way A's share of other costs is given in C15, while that of B is given in G15 as =1–C15. This means that any change in A's shares is immediately reflected in those of B, so that these do not have to be entered separately. Space costs for A are now entered in C18 as =C14*C7. The formulas for

Panel 2.2 Worksheet for a Simple Budget

	A	B	C	D	E	F	G
1	Budget						
2							
3	Space costs						
4	Apartment rent		875				
5	Heating costs		60				
6	Power		12				
7	Total Space costs		947				
8							
9	Other costs						
10	Groceries, meals		350				
11	Telephone rent		14				
12	Total other costs		364				
13							
14	Space costs for A		0.6		Space costs for B		0.4
15	Other costs for A		0.5		Other costs for B		0.5
16							
17	Costs for A				Costs for B		
18	Space costs		568.2		Space costs		378.8
19	Other costs		182		Other costs		182
20	Total		750.2		Total		560.8

C19, G18, and G19 are similar. Total costs for each person is the sum of the two kinds of costs, so that the content of C20 is =C18+C19.

Any desired change can now quickly be implemented. If the apartment rent in C4 is changed from $875 to $925, all values that depend on this cell are altered too, so that the results are immediately known. If the space cost shares are altered from 60% and 40% into 57.5% and 42.5%, only the value of C14 has to be changed into 0.575. The value of G14 then changes automatically to 0.425.

New items, such as newspapers and magazines, can be introduced by inserting a new row between rows 11 and 12, as explained in the next section.

2.2 Changing Columns and Rows

The presentation of the worksheet can be improved in a number of ways. In a blank worksheet, all columns, and therefore all cells, have the same width. But cells of the same worksheet are often used for widely varying purposes; some cells contain text and are used for descriptions or titles, which tend to be relatively lengthy, while numbers require less space. As mentioned previously, if text requires more space than the width of the cell, empty cells to the right are used. If there are no such cells, only the first part of the text that fits into the cell is displayed. This why in Panel 2.2 column B has been left empty.

Numbers may also require more space than provided by the cell width. If the space is not sufficient to format the contents properly, the cell display will consist of hash pound signs (######).

To change the cell width, the column width must be changed. Suppose that, because the descriptions in column A do not fit into the default cell width, the width of column A should be changed. This is done as shown in Panel 2.3. Using the mouse, the pointer is moved to the separation of the heading of the column to be extended with the next column. Pressing the (left) mouse button, this separation is dragged to the right until the desired width is obtained.

Panel 2.3 Changing the Column Width

	A	B
1	Budget	
2		
3	Space costs	

It is also possible to change the column width for number of columns at the same time by first selecting the columns concerned by dragging the cell pointer over the column headings. Then the column width of one of the columns is changed as described before, after which all selected columns will have the same width.

Since column B has become superfluous, it may be deleted. This is done by selecting that column and then choosing from the **Edit** menu the **Delete** command (Ctrl+K).

After a column has been deleted, the cell names in the columns to the right of the new column have all been changed. For example, the value of total other costs, which was stored in C12, is now found in B12. Any previous reference to C12 is changed automatically to B12. Multiple columns or one or more rows may be deleted in the same way by first selecting the corresponding heading(s) and then using the Delete command.

If any of the deleted cells are referenced to in other cells, these will display the message #REF! to indicate information is missing.

Turning back to the example, consider now adding the item Newspapers, etc. at $23 to the other costs in the budget. This is best done by inserting a new row above row 12, which is done by moving the pointer to a cell in row 12 and then selecting from the **Insert** menu the command **Rows**. Again all formulas of the sheet are adjusted automatically.

After the label "Newspapers, etc." has been entered in A12 and the value 23 in B12, cell B13 must be edited to include the term B12, so that its new content becomes:

=SUM(B10:B12)

It is possible to insert more than one row at a time by selecting a range of rows (by dragging the cell pointer over the row headings) that contains the number of rows that should be inserted. The new rows are inserted just above this range of rows.

A column is inserted in a similar way. More than one column may be inserted by first selecting a range of columns with the appropriate number of columns just to the right of the insertion point.

2.3 Ranges and Commands

Instead of dealing with a single cell, it is often useful to work with a rectangular block of cells. Such a block of cells is called a *range*. A range is indicated in a formula by its top left-hand cell and its bottom right-hand cell, joined by a colon. The top 2x4 rectangle of cells of the worksheet is designated as A1:B4. A range of cells is selected by dragging the cell pointer over the cells.

The most basic Microsoft® Excel commands can be accessed in a number of ways:

(1) by the buttons on the toolbars
(2) by keyboard shortcuts
(3) by the pull-down menus on the menubar.

In general, the toolbars give access to basic, frequently used commands, which have keyboard equivalents, while the menubar also contains more specialized and complicated commands.

A case in point is the command that deletes a cell or a range of cells. The demand is called **Cut** and it removes the content from the selected range of cells, keeping it stored to be pasted elsewhere, if that is desired. The command can be activated by the scissors button on the formatting toolbar, the keyboard shortcut Ctrl+X, or command **Cut** may be selected from the Edit menu.

A related command is the special keyboard key **Delete**, which deletes the cell content, but does not store it. The **Clear** and the **Delete** commands from the **Edit** menu do the same, but have more complicated subcommands.

Multiple access to the same commands gives the user a choice to select the most convenient mode of access. Buttons are easiest to use, but experienced users may prefer keyboard shortcuts.

2.4 Cell Formatting

Values or numbers can be represented or formatted in various ways. The default format of values is the *general* format, which represents numbers in as many decimal places as needed and as can be fitted within the available cell spaces and otherwise uses the scientific notation. The most important alternatives for economics and finance are the currency and the percentage formats.

The easiest way to change the format of a cell or a range of cells is to select it and then click the appropriate button on the formatting toolbar, see top part of Panel 2.4a.

Panel 2.4.a Number Cell Format Buttons

Panel 2.4b Number Submenu of Format Cells

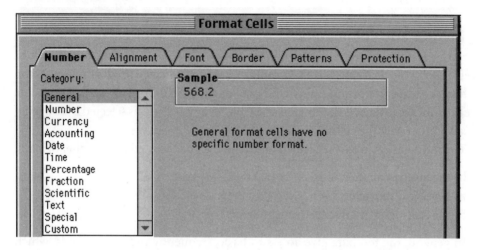

The currency format places a dollar sign ($) in front of the displayed number, the second expresses it in terms of percentages, and the third places a comma between groups of three digits, marking thousands, etc. The other two buttons are used to increase or decrease the number of digits of the display.

The formatting of numbers can also be performed choosing Cells from the Format menu, which gives access to many more formats, see Panel 2.4b, which displays the Number submenu. A wide variety of number formats is shown to be available. (Date and time formats are discussed later.)

Once a cell has been given the desired format, this format can be copied or 'painted' to other cells with the paintbrush button of the standard toolbar, see Panel 2.5a. First the cell from which the format is to be copied is selected, then the format painter button, and then the range to which the format should be copied is dragged. If the same format should be copied repeatedly, the paintbrush button should be double-clicked, and when finished, clicked again.

After all numbers have been formatted as required, the sheet has the appearance given in the worksheet in Panel 2.5d.

As indicated previously, instead of values, cells may contain text. Text is, as a default, *left aligned* which means that the text is displayed beginning at the left of each cell. Alternatively, the text may be *centered*, so that the text appears in the middle of the cell, or *right aligned*, with the text appearing as much as possible in spaces at the right of the cell. As mentioned in Chapter 1, numbers are by default aligned to the right. A change in alignment of numbers or text is obtained by using the relevant buttons of

Panel 2.5a Editing Toolbar

Panel 2.5b Formatting Toolbar

Panel 2.5c Font Toolbar

Panel 2.5d Formatted Budget Worksheet

	A	B	C	D	E
1	Budget				
2					
3	Space costs				
4	Apartment rent	$ 875			
5	Heating costs	$ 60			
6	Power	$ 12			
7	Total Space costs	$ 947			
8					
9	Other costs				
10	Groceries, meals	$ 350			
11	Telephone rent	$ 14			
12	Newspapers, etc.	$ 23			
13	Total other costs	$ 387			
14					
15	Space costs for A	60%		Space costs for B	40%
16	Other costs for A	50%		Other costs for B	50%
17					
18	Costs for A			Costs for B	
19	Space costs	$ 568		Space costs	$ 379
20	Other costs	$ 194		Other costs	$ 194
21	Total	$ 762		Total	$ 572

the formatting toolbar (see Panel 2.5b). Again, this is just a matter of selecting the cell or range of cells and clicking the suitable button. The button on the right is used to center the display over a number of columns.

We may also wish to change the appearance of letters and digits by making them **bold**, *italics*, or underlined. To do this, the corresponding buttons on the second row of Panel 2.5b may be used, which are toggles that turn a feature on and off.

The type of font and its size may be changed with the pull-down menu of the formatting toolbar (see Panel 2.5c). Note that changing the size of a font may change the row height.

The format painter button of the standard toolbar may be used to copy these formats, as indicated before. After a number of formatting changes, the Budget worksheet has the appearance given in Panel 2.6. In general it is advisable to spend not too much time and effort on spreadsheet appearance.

Panel 2.6 Worksheet after Further Formatting

	A	B	C	D	E
1		Budget			
2					
3	Space costs				
4	Apartment rent	$ 875			
5	Heating costs	$ 60			
6	Power	$ 12			
7	Total Space costs	$ 947			
8					
9	Other costs				
10	Groceries, meals	$ 350			
11	Telephone rent	$ 14			
12	Newspapers, etc.	$ 23			
13	Total other costs	$ 387			
14					
15	Space costs for A	60%		Space costs for B	40%
16	Other costs for A	50%		Other costs for B	50%
17					
18	Costs for A			Costs for B	
19	Space costs	$ 568		Space costs	$ 379
20	Other costs	$ 194		Other costs	$ 194
21	Total	$ 762		Total	$ 572

2.5 Moving and Copying
The space in the worksheet of Panel 2.6 is not used very efficiently, as the range D3:E13 is blank. A better use of space is obtained if the range of 'Other costs' is moved to the right of 'Space costs'. This can be done by first selecting the range A9:B13. After releasing the button, the pointer can be moved to the border of the selected range, where it changes to an arrow, as indicated in Panel 2.7.

Panel 2.7 Dragging a Range of Cells

9	Other costs		
10	Groceries, meals	$ 350	
11	Telephone rent	$ 14	
12	Newspapers, etc.	$ 23	
13	Total other costs	$ 387	

This range is then dragged to location (D3:E7), where it is dropped by releasing the mouse (see Panel 2.8). Rows 9–14, which are now empty, may be deleted by selecting the headings of these rows and using the **Delete** command of the **Edit** menu. The result is given in Panel 2.8. Note that the spreadsheet system automatically alters the references to cell names whose locations have changed.

Panel 2.8 The Rearranged Budget Worksheet

	A	B	C	D	E
1			**Budget**		
2					
3	Space costs			Other costs	
4	Apartment rent	$ 875		Groceries, meals	$ 350
5	Heating costs	$ 60		Telephone rent	$ 14
6	Power	$ 12		Newspapers, etc.	$ 23
7	Total Space costs	$ 947		Total other costs	$ 387
8					
9	Space costs for A	60%		Space costs for B	40%
10	Other costs for A	50%		Other costs for B	50%
11					
12	Costs for A			Costs for B	
13	Space costs	$ 568		Space costs	$ 379
14	Other costs	$ 194		Other costs	$ 194
15	Total	$ 762		Total	$ 572

Instead of dragging and dropping a selected range, it can, after selection, be cut using the **Cut** command (scissors button, shown in first row, first item of Panel 2.5, or the corresponding keyboard shortcut Ctrl+X). The selected range may then be pasted using the **Paste** (clipboard button, first row, third item of Panel 2.5 or Ctrl+V). Alternatively, the corresponding commands of the **Edit** menu can be employed.

If it is desirable to go back to a previous situation, the **Undo** button (leftward arrow in first row of Panel 2.5) can be used. The other arrow on this toolbar stands for **Redo**. Alternatively, the first commands of the **Edit** menu can be used. These Undo and Redo commands work for most changes. The Edit Undo and Redo command are grey, as opposed to black, if changes are not possible.

Worksheets can be very large and may contain many parts. Initially, it often seems that entering the contents of many cells requires a large amount of effort. However, since many parts of a spreadsheet are similar, they may be copied and then modified where needed.

The **Copy** command is used to copy a cell or a range of cells from one part of a worksheet to another, or from worksheet to worksheet in the same or in another workbook. This command is available in a number of ways. The simplest form of copying is a variant of drag and drop described above. The part to be copied is selected and the **Option** key is pressed down during the drag and drop action, which causes the original cell range to remain.

Alternatively, one of the three versions of the Copy and Paste commands may be used. If buttons are used, the procedure is as follows:

1. Select range of cells to be copied.
2. Click Copy button on the standard toolbar (first row, second item in Panel 2.5).
3. Select North-West corner of destination range.
4. Click Paste button of the standard toolbar (first row, third item in Panel 2.5).

Instead of the Copy button its keyboard shortcut **Ctrl+C** may be used, or the **Copy** command on the **Edit** menu. Instead of the Paste button its keyboard shortcut **Ctrl+V** may be used, or the **Paste** command on the **Edit** menu. There is also a short-cut menu which appears when holding down the control key and clicking on the selection.

In most cases the result from the copy and paste operations must be edited. For example, in the Budget worksheet the Costs for A in A12:B15 can be copied to D12:E15, but A in D12 should be changed to B. Furthermore, the amounts are not correct. This is related to the way the spreadsheet copies formulas which is discussed in the next section.

In some cases we may want to copy not the formula for a cell but just the *value* that it holds at the moment. For example, suppose we want to preserve in Panel 2.8 total costs for A and B when the rent is $925, regardless of the value of the rent and other costs. This is done by copying the range A12:D15, and selecting **Paste Special**, see Panel 2.9, from the **Edit** menu. After clicking on the Value and **OK** buttons, we obtain the result given in Panel 2.10. This action pastes just the values and not the formulas to another location, for example, the range A17:E20.

The values in this range do not change when, for example, the rent in B4 is changed. Since the display of a range with value pasted cells is the same as for cells that are linked, this can lead to serious errors if it is forgotten that these cells are not 'live'. For this reason this feature should be used only where there is a specific need for it.

In some cases it is desirable to have the transpose of a range, which means that rows and columns are interchanged. This is done by copying and then using the Transpose option from the Paste Special submenu. This will easily give unintended results if the range contains formulas with relative references. If the Values option is chosen in addition to the Transpose option, these problems are avoided. Panel 2.11 gives the result of using both options on the range A12:D15.

Panel 2.9 The Paste Special Submenu

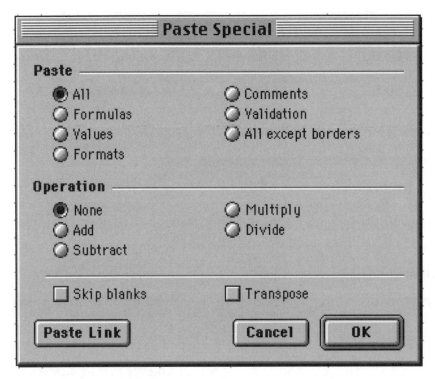

Panel 2.10 Pasting Values

17	Costs for A			Costs for B	
18	Space costs	$ 598		Space costs	$ 399
19	Other costs	$ 194		Other costs	$ 194
20	Total	$ 792		Total	$ 592

Panel 2.11 Transposition of a Range

	G	H	I	J
1	Costs for A	Space costs	Other costs	Total
2		$ 568	$ 194	$ 762
3				
4	Costs for B	Space costs	Other costs	Total
5		$ 379	$ 194	$ 572

Panel 2.12 Copying with Relative Cell References

	A	B	C	D
1	Price	Tax Perc.	Tax Amount	
2	$ 100.00	5%	$ 5.00	(=A2*B2)
3				
4	$ 150.00	5%	$ 7.50	(=A4*B4)

Panel 2.13 Copying with Absolute Row Reference

	A	B	C
6	Tax Perc.	5%	
7	Price	Tax Amount	
8	$ 100.00	$ 5.00	(=A8*B$6)
9	$ 150.00	$ 7.50	(=A9*B$6)

Panel 2.14 Formula Copying over Rows and Columns

	A	B	C	D	E	F
1	Price		$ 50	$ 60		
2						
3	Client	Quantities	Revenues			
4	A	10	$ 500	$ 600	(=$B4*C$1)	(=$B4*D$1)
5	B	30	$ 1,500	$ 1,800	(=$B5*C$1)	(=$B5*D$1)
6	C	20	$ 1,000	$ 1,200	(=$B6*C$1)	(=$B6*D$1)

2.6 Copying Formulas

As mentioned previously, this book confines itself to a brief introduction of basic spreadsheet features. However, certain features should be explained in some detail, because there are intricacies that are easily misunderstood without some systematic investigation. For this reason special attention is paid to the topic of *relative* and *absolute* cell references.

Consider Panel 2.12, which is concerned with the calculation of a sales tax amount by means of a simple multiplication. Cell C2 contains the formula =A2*B2. If cell C2 is copied to C4, that cell obtains the formula =A4*B4. While copying the formula, the system has automatically adjusted the row reference. If C2 was copied to D4, also the column reference would be adjusted, so that the resulting formula in D4 would be =B4*C4. Copying of formulas adjusts the formula automatically to the row and column of the new location. It interprets cell references in formulas *relatively*.

Panel 2.13 presents a slightly different situation. If cell B8 contained the formula =A8*B6, it would be copied to B9 as =A9*B7, which is not intended, since the row reference to B6 should not be adjusted. To prevent this adjustment, a dollar sign ($)

should be inserted in front of the row reference 6, so that the formula in B8 is =A8*B$6. Copying this formula to B9 leads to the intended result =A9*B$6. The row reference $6 is now an *absolute* reference.

Consider copying over both rows and columns. Panel 2.14 presents an example in which revenues of three quantities for prices of $50 and $60 should be calculated. The formula for C4 would be =B4*C1, but to enable copying this formula to the range C4:D6, column B in B4 should be made absolute, as well as row 1 in B1, so that the formula should be =$B4*C$1. After this formula is copied to C4:D6, the given numerical displays result (the formula displays are found in E4:F6.)

A handy shortcut exists for changing relative references to absolute ones and vice versa. After selection of the cell references in the control bar, select the F4 function key (Macintosh: Command T), which toggles the cell references through all possible positions.

Exercises

2.1 Start with the budget worksheet as displayed in Panel 2.2.

   (a) Format all money values as currency with 2 decimal places and the shares as percentages with 1 decimal place.

   (b) Delete columns B and F.

   (c) Change the width of each of the columns and make these as small as possible while making sure that there are at least two empty spaces between the displayed content of adjacent cells.

2.2. Person A has an annual income of $12,000 and person B of $9,500. Consider now the case in which other costs are shared in proportion to income. Modify the budget worksheet accordingly.

2.3. Using the Paste Special Value command, add to the budget worksheet rows containing the total costs for each person for all eight combinations of the following alternatives:

   (a) Apartment rent of $875 or $925.

   (b) Having newspaper and magazine subscriptions at $23 per month or not.

   (c) Person A paying 60% or 57.5% of space costs.

2.4 An alternative is considered with a third person, C, moving into an apartment with A and B having a rent of $1,150. Heating and power are consequently 30% higher, and food and meals costs are $500 per month. Space costs shares are: A 35%, B 35%, C 30%. Proceeding from the original budget worksheet, create a budget for this situation.

Assignments

2.1 Computer Purchase

You have bought by mail order a new computer, fax/modem, and printer. The price of the computer amounts to $1,995, the fax/modem $215, and the printer $565. A sales tax of 6% must be paid. Shipping per item is $5 plus 2% of the value, not including the sales tax. Purchase costs may be subtracted for income tax purposes, and your marginal tax rate is 42%.

Create an overview of the costs of the order, with rows for each item and a row for total amounts, and columns for price, sales tax, shipping and total, income tax saved, and effective costs. Give cells an appropriate format and adjust column width if necessary.

2.2 Tuition Fees

A foreign student wants to determine total tuition fees for a year of study at a Canadian university. The student intends to take 10 courses and course fees are $266 per course. The Students' Union Operating and Building Fee is $20, and the Students' Union Levy, $12.25. Both are compulsory. The Student Health Plan and the Student Dental Plan costs are $45 and $17.60, respectively, and are optional. Campus Recreation and Athletics costs are $17.60 and $21.50, respectively, and are compulsory. Create a spreadsheet file to determine the student's tuition fees, which includes for each item the quantity, its fee, and the total per item, and also overall total, in Canadian and US dollars (assume the exchange rate is C$1 = US$0.70). Use appropriate formatting.

2.3 Restaurant Meal

Go with a group to a restaurant for a meal. Create a worksheet which details each diner's share of the bill. Repeat if the group cannot agree.

2.4 Monthly Budget

Make a monthly budget for yourself using a spreadsheet. Assume that you are employed and have a take-home pay of $20,000 per year. You rent an apartment with costs of utilities not included. You have a car that must be replaced in a few years and you want to set aside money for annual savings and a holiday.

Group expenditures and calculate subtotals and percentages of take-home pay. Use appropriate row and column headers and select column widths and formats.

2.5 Currency Exchange Problem

You have a German bank account on which you receive every month an income of DM 1,500, which you want to transfer to your Canadian bank account. The funds can be automatically transferred periodically from the German account at a cost of 0.075% of the amount, with a minimum of DM 15 and a maximum of DM 100, plus a charge of C$10 from your Canadian bank. Assume that the exchange rate for 1 DM is about C$0.76. Your money in the German bank account earns no interest, while your money in the Canadian account can be utilized to yield 10% per year.

Determine how often (every 1, 2, 3, 4, 6, or 12 months) money should be transferred from your German bank account to your Canadian one in order to obtain a maximum return. Should income tax be taken into account?

Chapter 3
A Spreadsheet for a Project Budget

This chapter explains how a spreadsheet can be used to set up a budget for a project planned over a number of years with multiple partners and shows how information from this budget can be summarized. A number of important spreadsheet commands are introduced.

In this chapter you will learn the following spreadsheet commands and functions:

- Sheet Tabs
- Move, Copy, Delete, Insert Sheet
- Locked Cells
- Range Names
- Print
- Protection
- Goal Seek

3.1 Case Study Data and Requirements

The budgets considered in the previous chapter were simple and small. The advantages of spreadsheets become more obvious for larger and more complicated budgets, because spreadsheets are able to deal effortlessly with the involved structure of such budgets. But because of their size and complicated structure, large budget spreadsheets have to be carefully organized. To explain what is involved, a case study is used for which the following particulars are given.

The University of Calgary (UofC), Mount Royal College (MRC) and the Southern Alberta Institute of Technology (SAIT) are cooperating in Computer Assisted Learning for Economic Principles and are setting up a project for the development of software. They are cooperating with a commercial partner, Scientific SoftWare (SSW), which is taking part in the production and which will take care of the distribution to other educational institutions. For this purpose a project budget is needed.

The project has two stages, Year 1 and Year 2. In Year 1 a pilot project for computer assisted learning is set up and completed, to be used on a trial basis in the three educational institutions. Based on the results of the pilot project, the complete project is started and completed in Year 2, with large contributions of all partners. Separate budgets for the two years have to be set up, as well as a combined budget for the entire project.

Contributions to the project will be made by each of the three educational institutions, in the form of time allocated by its faculty members, and by SSW in the form of developers and computer programmers. In the budget the contributions of each partner should be given separately, as well as total project costs.

Project costs are described as follows. In Year 1 the UofC will supply a project coordinator for three months and each of the three institutions will supply two instructors for two months. The UofC will have one senior and one junior instructor, MRC one senior instructor and one instructor, and SAIT one instructor and one junior instructor. The salary for the coordinator is $6,500 per month, and salaries for senior instructors, instructors, and junior instructors are $6,000, $5,000, and $4,000 per month. On top of the salaries, 15% benefits have to be paid. SSW will contribute in the first year one month's work of a senior developer, one junior developer, and one systems analyst, who earn $7,000, $5,000, and $4,000 per month, respectively. Overhead for SSW personnel is 30%.

In Year 2, when most of the work is performed, the coordinator will work on the project for 9 months, of which 8 months are financed by the UofC and one month by SSW. The same instructors that were involved in Year 1, will work in Year 2 for 9 months, of which two months are financed by SSW. The same SSW personnel will work on the project for two months each.

A summary of the budget should be given for each contributor, both in terms of money and in terms of percentages of the total project costs.

The spreadsheet should be set up in such a way that any changes in some of the data (e.g. salary level) should be immediately reflected in the entire spreadsheet, including the summary.

3.2 Spreadsheet Organization

One way to deal with the organization of the spreadsheet is to improvise, while starting to build the main parts of the spreadsheet and reorganize parts of the sheet as needed. This usually works well but is time consuming. In most cases it is more efficient to start, after reading the data and requirements carefully, sketching the layout of the various parts of the spreadsheet. Only after the main decisions about the organization have been made should the actual building of the spreadsheet commence.

For the current case the following parts should be included:

1. The Data Section
   1.1. Main Budget Data
   1.2. Manpower Allocations
2. Budgets
   2.1. Budget Year 1
   2.2. Budget Year 2
   2.3. Total Budget
3. Summary
   3.1. Overview in Dollars
   3.2. Overview in Percentages

In larger spreadsheets such as the one for this case study it is advisable to include a *data section*, such as in Panel 3.1, which contains all or the most important data. There are two reasons for this. The first one is to make it easy to find the data on which the spreadsheet is based. If there is no data section, the data have to be traced in various locations. The second is to facilitate changing the data.

For example, we may wish to find out the consequences on the budget of changes in the monthly salary of instructors. If all items depending on this salary refer to the corresponding cell in the data section, a change in this cell will immediately lead to changes in the entire spreadsheet. We may even give this cell a name and use this name instead of the cell references in the parts of the spreadsheet depending on this cell.

For this project the most important data are the salaries of the faculty members and company personnel, the benefits and overhead percentages, and the manpower allocations. The latter indicate how many months the coordinator, the instructors, and the company staff will work and who will pay for the work. The resulting data, as entered in the spreadsheet, can be found in Panel 3.1.

The display of a sheet can be enhanced by using cell colors and borders. This is done by means of the command **Format, Cells, Patterns** and **Borders**. For example, light blue can be used for names of items, dark blue for headings, yellow for numerical data, and cream for numerical cells. Colors make it easier to obtain an overview. But as mentioned previously, spending too much time on formatting should be avoided.

Panel 3.1 Data Section for Budget

	A	B	C	D	E	F	G	H	I
1	Budget CAL Project								
2	Main Budget Data								
3	Coordinator	$6,600							
4	Senior Instructor	$8,000							
5	Instructor	$5,000							
6	Junior Instructor	$4,000							
7	Senior Developer	$7,000							
8	Junior Developer	$6,000							
9	Systems Analyst	$4,000							
10	Ben. Ac. Staff (BE)	15%							
11	Overhead (OH)	30%							
12									
13	Manpower Allocations								
14	Partner	UofC	MRC	SAIT	SSW	UofG	MRC	BAIT	BSW
15		Year 1				Year 2			
16	Coordinator	3	0	0	0	8	0	0	1
17	Senior Instructor	2	2	0	0	7	7	0	2
18	Instructor	0	2	2	0	0	7	7	2
19	Junior Instructor	2	0	2	0	7	0	7	2
20	Senior Developer	0	0	0	1	0	0	0	2
21	Junior Developer	0	0	0	1	0	0	0	2
22	Systems Analyst	0	0	0	1	0	0	0	2

3.3 Workbook and Sheets

The Excel spreadsheet consists of a workbook with a number of sheets.. The default number of sheets in a workbook is three, with names Sheet1, Sheet2, and Sheet3 written on the tabs below the sheet. A mouse click on the tab gives access to the corresponding sheet, but also the keyboard can be used to go to an adjacent sheet with **Ctrl+Page Down(Up)**(Windows) or **Command+Page Down(Up)**(Macintosh). A double click on the tab allows alteration of the sheet name. The default number of sheets is changed via the menu **Tools, Preferences, General**. If the sheet tabs are not visible, the command **Tools Preferences, View, Sheet Tabs** should be used.

Sheets can be rearranged or copied by means of the command **Edit, Move** or **Copy Sheet**. Sheets are deleted with the command **Edit, Delete Sheet** and new sheets inserted using the command **Insert, Worksheet**.

Cell references such as A1 refer to cell A1 on the same sheet. To refer to a cell on another sheet, the reference to that cell should be preceded by the sheet name followed by "!". For example, in Sheet2, cell A1 of Sheet1 is referenced as Sheet1!A1.

A good place for the data section is on the first sheet of the workbook. For this project the three following sheets are used for the budgets of Years 1 and 2 and the total budget, while the summary is entered on the first sheet together with the data section. The sheet tabs of the workbook, after renaming, are as displayed at the bottom of Panel 3.1.

When a workbook is organized, the following questions should be answered:

1. How should the material be organized in terms of sheets?
2. How should each sheet be organized?

General criteria for good arrangements are:

1. The resulting format must seem logical to the user.
2. The content of each screen should contain as much information as possible that belongs together.
3. The content of each printed page should contain as much information as possible that belongs together.

As both the screen content and the printed page content depend on column width and row height, and these depend on the cell content in terms of spaces and letter type, determining the best organization of a spreadsheet can be complicated. It is generally advisable to spend some time and effort on spreadsheet appearance and organization, but since appearance is less important than content, the temptation to spend too much time on appearance should be resisted. It is of importance to develop good habits and standard formats.

3.4 Building the Project Budget Spreadsheet

The building of the actual budgets will now be described, starting with the Budget for Year 1 on Sheet2, which is renamed as BudgetY1, while Sheet1 is renamed as Data&Sum.

The budget has a number of items that are paid by the various partners. As there are only four partners in the project but many items, it is decided to use columns for partners and rows for items, as relatively few columns but many rows are visible on one screen (see Panel 3.2).

The actual building of the spreadsheet starts with the detailed budget for Year 1. This budget uses column A for descriptions and the next five columns for the amounts to be contributed by the partners and the totals: UofC, MRC, SAIT, SSW and the Total (see Panel 3.2 for the number display and Panel 3.3 for the formula display).

The content of cell B3 is the number of months worked by the coordinator times the corresponding salary, which is Data&Sum!B3*Data&Sum!B16, but since this cell may be used for copying downwards and to the right, we may enter into it =Data&Sum!$B3*Data&Sum!B16, so that the column in B3 does not shift while copying. Cell B3 should be given the appropriate number format, as this is copied along with the formula. After this, B3 may be copied to B3:E9. Note that to achieve these results, rows and columns of the data and the budget should correspond with each other. The data have, of course, been arranged accordingly.

Panel 3.2 Budget for Year 1 (Number Display)

	A	B	C	D	E	F
1	**Budget Year 1**					
2	Partner	UofC	MRC	SAIT	SSW	Total
3	Coordinator	$ 19,500	$ –	$ –	$ –	$ 19,500
4	Senior Instructor	$ 12,000	$ 12,000	$ –	$ –	$ 24,000
5	Instructor	$ –	$ 10,000	$ 10,000	$ –	$ 20,000
6	Junior Instructor	$ 8,000	$ –	$ 8,000	$ –	$ 16,000
7	Senior Developer	$ –	$ –	$ –	$ 7,000	$ 7,000
8	Junior Developer	$ –	$ –	$ –	$ 5,000	$ 5,000
9	Systems Analyst	$ –	$ –	$ –	$ 4,000	$ 4,000
10	Ac. Sal. w/o Ben.	$ 39,500	$ 22,000	$ 18,000	$ –	$ 79,500
11	Benefits Ac. Staff	$ 5,925	$ 3,300	$ 2,700	$ –	$ 11,925
12	Total Ac. Costs	$ 45,425	$ 25,300	$ 20,700	$ –	$ 91,425
13	Dev. Cost w/o Ov.	$ –	$ –	$ –	$ 16,000	$ 16,000
14	Overhead	$ –	$ –	$ –	$ 4,800	$ 4,800
15	Total Dev. Costs	$ –	$ –	$ –	$ 20,800	$ 20,800
16	Total Costs	$ 45,425	$ 25,300	$ 20,700	$ 20,800	$112,225
17	Contribution %	40%	23%	18%	19%	100%

Panel 3.3 Budget for Year 1 (Formula Display)

	A	B
1	**Budget Year 1**	
2	Partner	UofC
3	Coordinator	='Data&Sum'!$B3*'Data&Sum'!B16
4	Senior Instructor	='Data&Sum'!$B4*'Data&Sum'!B17
5	Instructor	='Data&Sum'!$B5*'Data&Sum'!B18
6	Junior Instructor	='Data&Sum'!$B6*'Data&Sum'!B19
7	Senior Developer	='Data&Sum'!$B7*'Data&Sum'!B20
8	Junior Developer	='Data&Sum'!$B8*'Data&Sum'!B21
9	Systems Analyst	='Data&Sum'!$B9*'Data&Sum'!B22
10	Ac. Sal. w/o Ben.	=SUM(B3:B6)
11	Benefits Ac. Staff	=BE*B10
12	Total Ac. Costs	=SUM(B10:B11)
13	Dev. Cost w/o Ov.	=SUM(B7:B9)
14	Overhead	=OH*B13
15	Total Dev. Costs	=SUM(B13:B14)
16	Total Costs	=B12+B15
17	Contribution %	=B16/$F$16

The academic salaries without benefits in cell B10 contains the sum of the cells B3:B6. The benefits in cell B11 are equal to the salary total times the benefit percentage, which is BE*B10 (the cell name BE is explained below). The total in B12 is the sum of B10:B11.

The part referring to company personnel is treated in the same manner, with B13, which represents Development Costs without Overhead, containing the sum of B7:B9, Overhead costs in B14 containing OH*B13, where OH is the name of the overhead percentage cell, B15 giving Total Development Costs, and B16 Total Costs.

As the formulas for MRC, SAIT, and SSW are similar to those for UofC, the range B3:B16 is copied to C3:E16. The costs over all four units are given by the range F3:F16 which contain the obvious summation formulas.

Of the total for the first year, $112,225 in cell F16, we wish to indicate the percentages of the partners. Cell B17 is therefore given the formula =B16/$F16, which is copied to the range C17:F17.

Once the budget for Year 1 has been completed, the budget for Year 2 can easily be obtained by copying the sheet BudgetY1 to another sheet using the command **Edit**, **Move** or **Copy Sheet**, and changing the cell content where necessary.

The Total Project Budget is found by copying the sheet for Year 1 or Year 2 to a new sheet for Year 1 or 2, then defining one cell value as the sum of the corresponding cells of the budgets for Year 1 and Year 2, which means that cell B3 is given the formula =BudgetY1!B3+BudgetY2!B3 and then copying this formula (with its relative cell references) to all other value cells.

As persons perusing these budgets may wish to concentrate their attention on totals and relative contributions, a budget summary is required, both in dollar amounts and in percentages, giving the contributions of the four partners over the two years and the total budget. These summaries, which are best placed close to the data in the Data&Sum sheet are given in Panel 3.4. The formulas for the amounts part refer to the corresponding parts of the complete budgets, so that cell E5 has the formula =BudgetY1!E16, which is copied to E5:I5. The other parts are made up in a similar way.

3.5 Cell and Range Names

Names for cells such as AQ142 and ranges such as X45:AD67 are difficult to remember. It is possible, however, to assign names for cells and ranges that are more easily recalled. These names may then be used in formulas or for printing commands.

Names can be defined by first selecting the cell or the range, and then using the command **Insert**, **Name**, **Define**, or {Command} L. The resulting menu lists previously defined names.

For example, we may give cell B10, the Benefits Ac. Staff percentage, the name BE. After this has been done, this name may be used in cell BudgetY1!B11, with the formula =BE*B10. If a name is copied, the absolute location (and not the relative one as in Lotus 123) is copied. Likewise, the entire range for the Summary, D2:I12 may be named SUMMARY. This can be useful for printing purposes. Names are not sensitive to case, so that BE and be indicate the same location.

Panel 3.4 Budget Summary

	A	B	C	D	E	F	G	H	I
1	Budget CAL Project			Summary					
2	Main Budget Data			Amounts					
3	Coordinator	10,500		Partner	UofC	MRC	SAIT	SSW	Total
4	Senior Instructor	$8,000		Year 1	$ 45,425	$ 25,300	$ 20,700	$ 20,800	$112,225
5	Instructor	$6,000		Year 2	$140,300	$ 88,550	$ 72,450	$ 83,575	$384,875
6	Junior Instructor	$4,000		Total	$185,725	$113,850	$ 93,150	$104,375	$497,100
7	Senior Developer	$7,000		%					
8	Junior Developer	$5,000		Partner	UofC	MRC	SAIT	SSW	Total
9	Systems Analyst	$4,000		Year 1	9%	5%	4%	4%	23%
10	Ben. Ac. Staff (BE)	15%		Year 2	29%	18%	15%	17%	77%
11	Overhead (OH)	30%		Total	37%	23%	19%	21%	100%
12									
13	Manpower Allocations								
14	Partner	UofC	MRC	SAIT	SSW	UofC	MRC	SAIT	SSW
15		Year 1				Year 2			
16	Coordinator	3	0	0	0	8	0	0	1
17	Senior Instructor	2	2	0	0	7	7	0	2
18	Instructor	0	2	2	0	0	7	7	2
19	Junior Instructor	2	0	2	0	7	0	7	2
20	Senior Developer	0	0	0	1	0	0	0	2
21	Junior Developer	0	0	0	1	0	0	0	2
22	Systems Analyst	0	0	0	1	0	0	0	2

3.6 Printing the Spreadsheet

The printing commands can be found under the **File** menu, of which **Page Setup**, **Print Preview** and **Print** are the most important. The spreadsheet may be printed in a variety of ways. First the area of the sheet to be printed can be selected, after which, if the area does not fit on one page, the pages are printed in the order of first going down and then to the right. The default is to print gridlines but not row and column headings.

All printing related defaults can be changed using, from the **File** menu, the **Page Setup** dialog box, with its four tabs: Page, Margin, Header/Footer, and Sheet (see Panel 3.5). First we may change which part of the sheet is printed using the Sheet tab. For example, suppose we wish to print the budget for Year 1, which is found in the range BudgetY1!A1:F17. This range is entered in the Print Area box either by the keyboard or by selecting this area by the mouse. (The Page setup menu itself may make this less easy to accomplish, but it can be moved by the mouse.) The Print options such as gridlines and Row and Column Headings may be indicated as desired. If the selected area is too large to fit on one page, it may be fit on one or more pages by scaling down the print, with Page Tab menu. Using the Page Setup menu, almost any desired printing format can be obtained.

Panel 3.5 The Page Setup Menu

3.7 Worksheet Protection

Spreadsheets are sometimes given to other persons to enter or change data. Other parts of the spreadsheet may be changed inadvertently by their actions. This is not a disaster when a copy of the spreadsheet has been saved, but it can lead to incorrect conclusions. In such cases the *protection* feature can be used, which makes it impossible to change certain cells.

By default, the entire sheet and the entire workbook are *unprotected*, which means that all cells can be altered. Each cell is either *locked* or not. By default all cells are locked. When a sheet or workbook is protected, locked cells cannot be altered. The protection of a sheet or workbook can be altered by the **Protection** item of the **Tools** menu. Cells can be locked or unlocked by means of the command **Format, Cell, Protection** submenu. The protection may be made secure by a password.

3.8 Data and Results

One of the main advantages of the spreadsheet over the written page is that changes can be made which are instantly implemented, so that the results are immediately available. In this case, the data are the salaries, percentages, and manpower schedules, and the results are given by the summary, which all appear on the Data&Sum sheet. For example, it may be desirable to limit the amount of SSW, which is currently $104,375 to $100,000. This can be done by varying the Overhead percentage, which is 30%, downwards.

The variation can be done by trial and error, changing cell B11 until cell H7 equals $100,000. However, the spreadsheet has a special command **Goal Seek** from the **Tools** menu. First H7 is selected, then the command is invoked, which results in the Goal Seek menu, see Panel 3.6.

Panel 3.6 The Goal Seek Menu

After entering $100,000 and B11, and clicking OK, the desired result given in Panel 3.7 is obtained.

Panel 3.7 Means and Goals for the Software Project

	A	B	C	D	E	F	G	H	I
1	Budget CAL Project			Summary					
2	Main Budget Data			Amounts					
3	Coordinator	$6,500		Partner	UofC	MRC	SAIT	SSW	Total
4	Senior Instructor	$6,000		Year 1	$ 46,425	$ 26,300	$ 20,700	$ 10,342	$110,767
5	Instructor	$5,000		Year 2	$140,300	$ 86,550	$ 72,450	$ 80,858	$361,858
6	Junior Instructor	$4,000		Total	$185,725	$113,850	$ 93,150	$100,000	$492,725
7	Senior Developer	$7,000		%					
8	Junior Developer	$5,000		Partner	UofC	MRC	SAIT	SSW	Total
9	Systems Analyst	$4,000		Year 1	9%	5%	4%	4%	22%
10	Ben. Ac. Staff (BE)	15%		Year 2	28%	18%	15%	16%	78%
11	Overhead (OH)	21%		Total	38%	23%	19%	20%	100%

Exercises

3.1. Change some of the data to keep the budget total under $450,000.

3.2. Assume there is an inflation of 5% per year, so that all salaries are 5% higher in Year 2. Include this in the budget.

3.3. Increase the benefit percentage for academic staff to 30% by intervals of 5%. Find the corresponding total budget amounts by replacing the formula with its calculated value.

Assignments

3.1 Golf Club Case

You are taking care of the administration of a golf club and your task is to make up the bills of its 10 members for last month and to find the various total amounts over all members.

The monthly fee for full members is $40 and for student members $20. The golf fee per hour on weekends is $9 and on weekdays, $6. Students get a discount on golf fees of 25%. Beer costs $2 and wine $10, but students get a discount of 10%.

Member	Status	Golf W/end	Golf W/day	Beer	Wine
Addington	1	0	4	0	1
Armstrong	0	2	2	3	1
Askew	0	4	5	0	2
Balash	1	0	0	3	0
Barton	0	2	0	4	0
Bennett	1	0	4	2	0
Beres	1	0	4	0	0
Blackwell	0	3	4	3	1
Blampied	1	6	0	0	2
Bouchard	0	5	5	0	0

The following data are known (0 = full member, 1 = student member).
Enter the data into a spreadsheet.
(a) Find the totals for the monthly billing for the entire club.
(b) Make up the monthly bills for each of the members on separate sheets using the copy command in an efficient manner.
(c) Using the Paste Special command, give the total billing if
  (i) students do not get any discounts;
  (ii) instead of the student discounts everybody pays $30 membership, the golf fees are discounted by 10% and the beer and wine prices by 5%;
  (iii) all student members leave.

3.2 Hospital Cutbacks

You are helping out with formulating the annual budget for hospitals of the Department of Health of the Province. There are 10 hospitals, for which the following data in the coming year are known (1 = emergency department., 0 = no emergency department).

Hospital	Emergency Department	Acute PD	NHPD	OutPatient Days	Outpatient Visits
Winter Valley	1	100,000	0	3,000	5,000
St. Mary	1	50,000	20,000	2,000	6,000
Grasslands	0	20,000	25,000	1,000	4,500
Mountain View	1	75,000	10,000	2,500	2,400
Yellow River	0	60,000	30,000	5,000	1,500
Crossroads	0	30,000	15,000	2,000	2,700
Main	1	150,000	0	1,000	700
Athabasca	0	10,000	5,000	4,200	1,200
Ft St. James	0	5,600	6,000	1,300	340
Red Creek	1	89,000	42,000	6,000	1,100

To set the budget for each hospital, the following data are used. A hospital with an emergency department receives a lump sum of $2,000,000, and those without, $1,000,000. Acute care patient days will be paid with $350, and nursing home patient days with $150. An outpatient day is worth $75 and an outpatient visit $40, but hospitals with an emergency department receive an extra 10% for outpatient days and visits.

Enter the data into a spreadsheet and use a separate data section.

(a) Make up the total annual hospital budget.

(b) Make up a budget for each hospital stating the prices and quantities using the copy command in an efficient manner, using the Paste Special Transpose command.

(c) Using the Paste Special command, give the total billing if
(i) Emergency hospitals do not get the extra 10%.
(ii) If, in addition to the above, all acute and nursing home patient days are given 10% less.
(iii) If, in addition to the above, the lump sums are decreased by $50,000.

Chapter 4
Graphs and Charts

This chapter introduces the construction of graphs or charts with Excel. After some remarks about the importance of graphical representation, the various types of charts are discussed with as example the GDP per capita of a number of economic units. Scatter graphs and the related regression lines and equations are treated.

In this chapter you will learn the following spreadsheet commands and functions:

- Chart
- Chart Wizard
- Add Trendline

4.1 Introduction

A spreadsheet is a tool for working with numbers. Numbers have the advantage that they can be used in computations and can be compared in numerous ways, but visually they are not very exciting. To attract the attention of, and provide information to, eyes and minds that are forever scanning the environment, numbers that are deemed to be important must be transformed in graphs or charts, which allow a quick estimate of relative sizes and possible relationships.

Hence, charts are used for display purposes, which means that careful attention should be paid to details such as size, type of chart, titles, legends, fonts, colors, and shading. The kind of presentation for which the chart is used also plays a role. A chart to be viewed in an oral presentation to an audience should be less complicated and easy to understand than one to be studied in a book or on a computer screen by an unhurried viewer.

The original Lotus spreadsheet was called Lotus 1-2-3 because it contained (1) a spreadsheet, (2) graphical tools, and (3) database tools. The graphical features of the current Excel spreadsheet enable the construction of graphs of many types in a fast and convenient manner.

Many kinds of charts exist, and Excel includes most of the common types. In this chapter only the most important types of charts and their features will be treated, but the Chart Wizard provides fast access to charts of all types.

4.2 The Simple Column Chart

Charting is best introduced by examples, and to illustrate the basic default column graph, data are used for the 1995 Gross Domestic Product (GDP) per capita in US dollars for some countries and economic entities published by the Organization for Economic Cooperation and Development (OECD), see Panel 4.1.

Two values are given for GDP per capita, one based on conversion to US dollars using exchange rates, and the other determined by the purchasing power of the monetary unit concerned compared to the purchasing power of the US dollar in the USA. The data are ordered according to decreasing GDP per capita using exchange rates. Column B contains convenient abbreviations of the six economic units to be used in the following.

Panel 4.1 GDP per Capita Data

	A	B	C	D
			EXCHR	PPP
1			EXCHR	PPP
2	JAPAN	JAP	$ 40,726	$ 21,795
3	UNITED STATES	USA	$ 26,438	$ 26,438
4	EUROPEAN UNION	EUN	$ 22,631	$ 18,609
5	AUSTRALIA	AUS	$ 19,314	$ 19,354
6	CANADA	CAN	$ 18,915	$ 21,031
7	MEXICO	MEX	$ 2,946	$ 7,383

The process of generating a graph, which Excel calls a *chart*, can be very automatic. The default type of chart is a *column chart*, which is obtained by selecting the range containing the data and then pressing the key F11. If the range B2:C7 of Panel 4.1 is selected, this results in a new sheet, called Chart 1, inserted before the current sheet, on which the chart is displayed (see Panel 4.2).

Panel 4.2 The Default Column Format

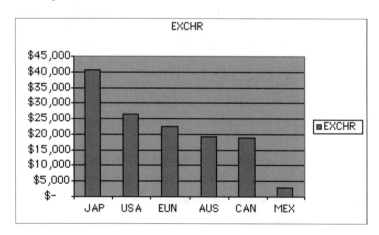

In the default column chart the data in the first column of the selected area are used as labels for the X- or *category* axis, while the data in the second column are graphed on the Y-axis of which the scale has the same currency format as this second column. This Y-axis has grid lines. In the default chart format there is the automatically generated legend EXCHR, which the spreadsheet takes from cell C1. To

Chart Wizard icon

Panel 4.3 Step 1 of the Chart Wizard

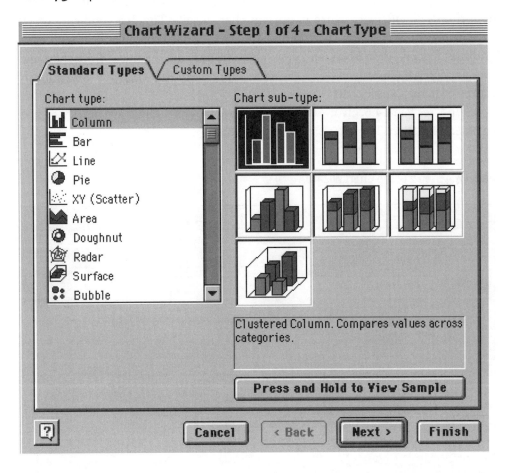

remove it, it should be selected with the mouse, after which the **Delete** key is pressed or the **Edit**, **Clear All** command is used.

The default format of this chart may not be precisely what is wanted. For example, the size may be too large, or the chart should be embedded close to the data and on the same sheet. To generate a chart with different features, the **Chart Wizard** may be used, which is activated, after selecting the data, by clicking its icon, see top of Panel 4.3.

The various steps (4) of the Chart Wizard then appear. Step 1, see Panel 4.3, gives the opportunity to select the chart type, with the type most likely to be suitable highlighted, in this case the column chart. A subtype of this chart can be chosen from the displayed examples. As these subtypes deal with the display of multiple series, they are not relevant here. The resulting chart can be viewed by pressing the button 'Press and Hold to View Sample'.

After the **Next** button is pressed, Step 2 appears, see Panel 4.4, which gives a preliminary version of the chart, together with an opportunity to select or reselect the data, and change the interpretation in terms of rows and columns.

Pressing the **Next** button again, results in Step 3, see Panel 4.5, which gives the opportunity to enter or change important chart details. The first submenu allows entering of the title of the chart and of the axes. Other submenus deal with axes, gridlines, legends, data labels, and data tables. In this case the titles of the chart and axes are entered, and the existing legend is suppressed. Any change is immediately expressed in the sample chart.

Step 4, see Panel 4.6, involves the placement of the chart, either as a new sheet or as an object on a sheet. The latter is chosen in this case.

Panel 4.4 Step 2 of the Chart Wizard

Panel 4.5 Step 3 of the Chart Wizard

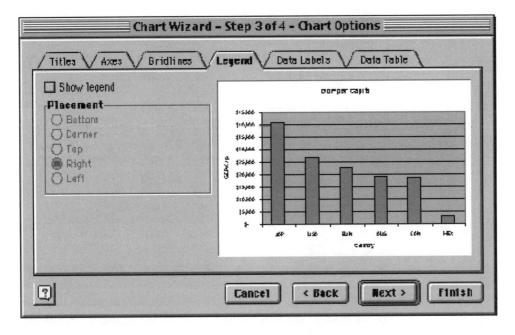

Panel 4.6 Step 4 of the Chart Wizard

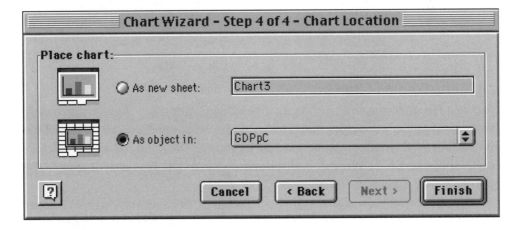

Panel 4.7 The Final Result with Selected Chart

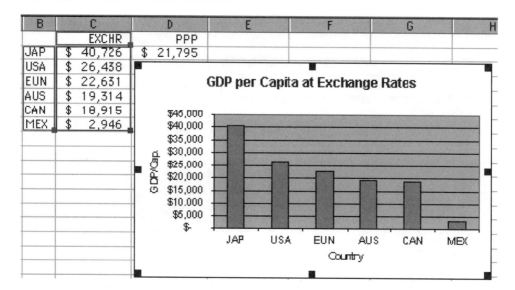

Panel 4.7 gives the final result, which has the desired smaller size as well as titles for the chart and the Y-axis. The chart is linked to the highlighted data, and any change in these data will be immediately reflected in the chart.

The chart has tiny square handles, which means that it is *selected*, so that these handles may be used to change its size. As long as it is selected, the chart may be deleted by means of the **Delete** key or the command **Edit, Clear All** or copied to another place, for example, a word processing document. The chart selection is undone by clicking outside the chart. The chart is selected again by clicking once on it, after which it can be deleted or resized as indicated before. The various parts of the chart may be *selected* by clicking on the part. Double-clicking the part concerned results in a menu that allows making the desired changes.

4.3 Group Column Charts

Now, in addition to the GDP per capita for exchange rates, the series for purchasing Power Parity (PPP) will be graphed. This is done by selecting the range B1:D7, which also includes the headings, to be used as legends in the chart. The default chart obtained by the **Chart Wizard**, is displayed in Panel 4.8. This chart includes the appropriate legends.

The chart conveys the information that, though Japan has a much higher GDP per capita than other economic units for exchange rate conversion, the results for purchasing power conversion are about the same as those for the other units, except Mexico. Obtaining this information from the numbers requires more effort and concentration.

In the data for GDP per capita the series were placed in columns, which Excel had to guess. Now a case is considered in which the data can be interpreted as being

Panel 4.8 The Default Chart for Two Series

	B	C	D	E	F
1		EXCHR	PPP		
2	JAP	$ 40,726	$ 21,795		
3	USA	$ 26,438	$ 26,438		
4	EUN	$ 22,631	$ 18,609		
5	AUS	$ 19,314	$ 19,354		
6	CAN	$ 18,915	$ 21,031		
7	MEX	$ 2,946	$ 7,383		

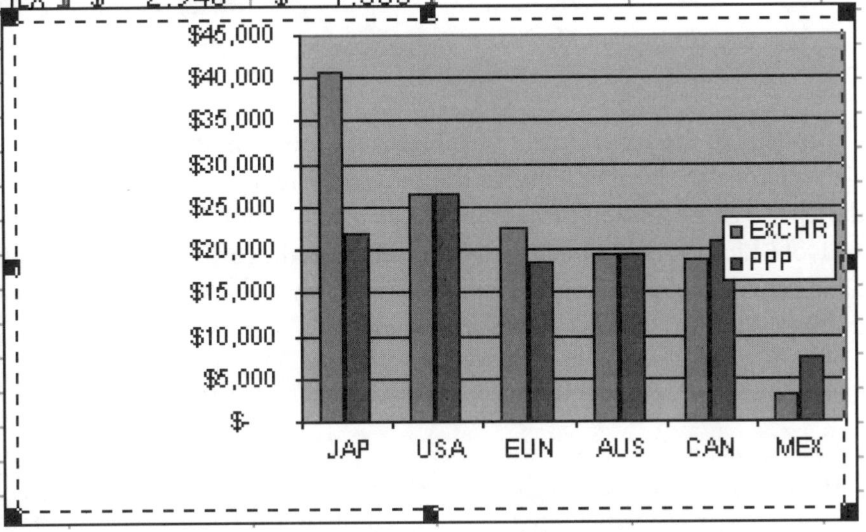

Panel 4.9 Summary of Results for the Joint Budget Case

	A	B	C	D	E	F
1	Summary					
2	Amounts					
3	Partner	UofC	MRC	SAIT	SSW	Total
4	Year 1	$ 21,330	$ 11,880	$ 9,720	$ 36,800	$ 79,730
5	Year 2	$ 140,300	$ 88,550	$ 72,450	$ 115,575	$ 416,875
6	Total	$ 161,630	$ 100,430	$ 82,170	$ 152,375	$ 496,605

arranged in rows or in columns. For this purpose the summary of results for the joint budget of Chapter 3 is used, see Panel 4.9.

The range A3:E5 is selected, after which the Chart Wizard is activated. The resulting default chart is illustrated on the left-hand side of Panel 4.10. The reason is that the number of numeric rows is less than the number of columns, so that a row arrangement of the data is more likely to be desirable. If in Step 2 of the Chart Wizard the option *Series in Columns* is chosen, the chart displayed on the right-hand side in Panel 4.10 results.

Panel 4.10 Default Column Charts for Row and Column Data Arrangement

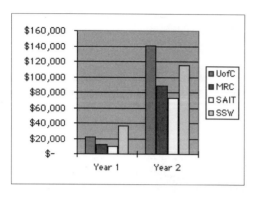 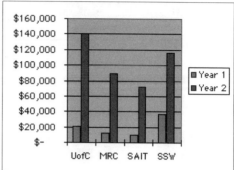

Instead of the arrangement of columns next to each other, they may be stacked. This type of chart is called a *stacked column chart*. This chart can be chosen in Step 1 of the Chart Wizard, option 3 (see Panel 4.3, chart sub-type). The result is given in Panel 4.11, of which the chart on the left-hand side gives the row series result and the right-hand side the column series result. Stacked column charts are used when separate numbers should be compared with their total.

Panel 4.11 Stacked Column Charts for Row and Column Data Arrangement

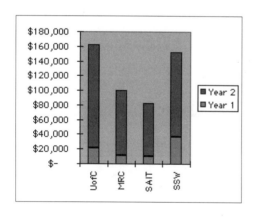 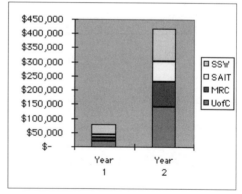

4.4 Bar Charts

Interchange of X- and Y-axis of a column chart results in a *bar chart*. Such a chart is obtained by selecting in Step 1 of the Chart Wizard the option in the second position (see Panel 4.3). The result is given in Panel 4.12 for GDP per Capita, with PPP conversion. It is an alternative to the column chart of Panel 4.7.

Panel 4.12 Bar Chart for GDP per Capita, PPP Conversion

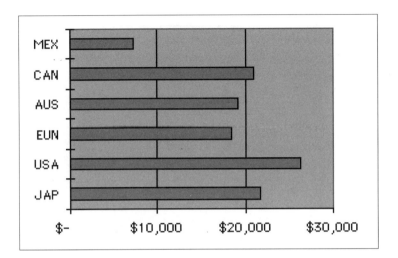

A possible advantage of this chart over the column chart is its aspect, which is the height width ratio, because it is less high than wide, which is a desirable feature of a chart. A chart may be given any rectangular shape, but the bars or columns should not become too thin.

4.5 Line Charts

In line charts the columns are replaced by points at the same height which are linked by lines. These charts are generated by selecting the third option in step 1 of the Chart Wizard. The points may be displayed by a symbol (diamond, square, etc.), see Panel 4.13. In column and bar charts the data displayed on the X-axis are usually labels identifying different units, e.g. countries in the example, though numbers may also be used. Since a line suggests continuity between adjacent points, a line chart would not be appropriate for an X-axis representing countries as in the example. It is, however, useful if the data on X-axis data represent time periods. It should be realized that the X-axis data are not plotted, but simply spaced over the X-axis in the same order as they appear in the data. For plotting numerical data along the X-axis, scatter charts should be used (see below).

An appropriate example of a line chart is provided by Panel 4.13, which displays quarterly gasoline sales in Alberta. The chart suggests that, in addition to a seasonal fluctuation, there is a slight downward trend in gasoline sales over time.

The trend line involved may be generated by making the chart active by clicking on it, after which the main menu **Data** commands (to the right of the Tools commands) change into **Chart commands**. This contains the **Add Trendline** command, which, when invoked, results in the menu displayed in Panel 4.14. In this case a linear trend seems to apply.

Panel 4.13 Line Chart for Quarterly Gasoline Sales

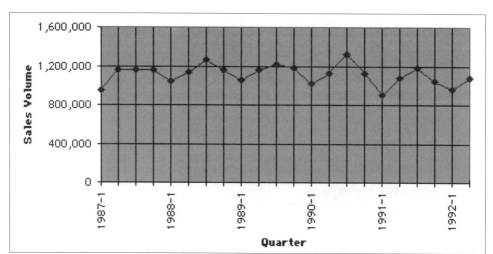

Panel 4.14 The Add Trendline Menu

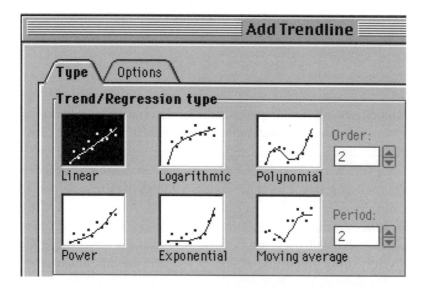

From the Options submenu the **Display equation** and **Display r-squared value** boxes are checked. The result is the trend line displayed in Panel 4.15. There is indeed a slight negative trend. The estimates are based on least squares regression.

There is a variant of the line chart, which fills in the space under the line. This is called an *area chart* and it is obtained by selecting in Step 1 of the Chart Wizard the fifth type, or by using, after having made the chart active, the **Chart, Chart Type** command. The result is given in Panel 4.16 and is a sort of cross of column and line charts. This chart is a bit more vivid than the line chart, so that it may be useful when that is needed.

Panel 4.15 Trend Line for Quarterly Gasoline Sales

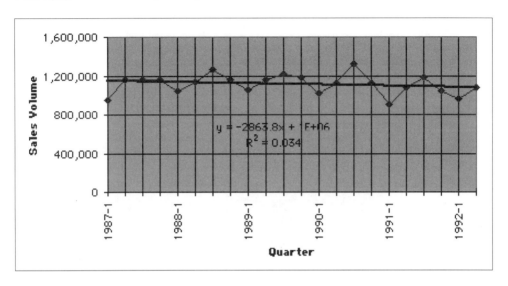

Panel 4.16 Area Chart for Quarterly Gasoline Sales

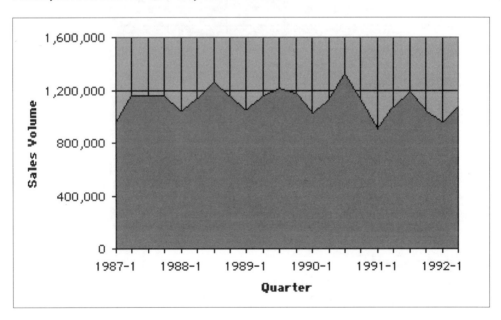

Panel 4.17 Scatter Chart for GDPs at Exchange Rate and Purchasing Power Parities

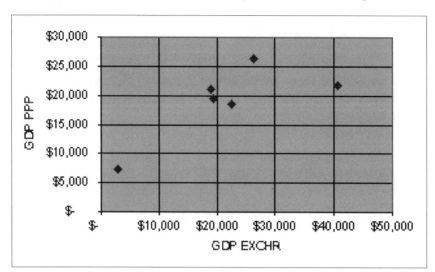

Panel 4.18 Scatter Chart with Trendline

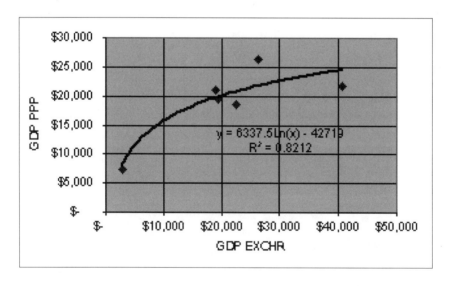

4.6 Scatter Charts

The chart in Panel 4.8 suggests that countries with a large GDP per capita for exchange rate conversion have smaller GDPs per capita for PPP conversion, and the reverse is true for countries with a small GDP per capita. Such a tendency may become more obvious if the GDPs per capita for PPP are plotted against those for exchange rates. Such plotting is done in a *scatter chart*, which can be selected in Step 1 of the Chart Wizard menu. The default option seems appropriate. After addition of axes titles and X-axis gridlines, the chart given in Panel 4.17 results.

There seems indeed to be a nonlinear relationship between the two kinds of GDP data. The PPP GDP is higher than the ER GDP for low ER GDP and lower for high ER GDP. This relationship can be estimated using the command **Chart, Add Trendline** after having made the chart active.

This trendline can be estimated by a regression as indicated before. This time the logarithmic option seems appropriate. The resulting trend line, as well as the regression equation and the R2 are given in Panel 4.18. The correlation is fairly high.

The same chart may be generated using a more complete data set for all the countries of the OECD. The result is displayed in Panel 4.19, which indicates that there is indeed a strong relationship in the sense that richer countries tend to have higher prices.

Panel 4.19 Trendline Scatter Chart for Complete Data Set

4.7 Pie Charts

Pie charts express each numerical entry in the data as a percentage of the total and draw a pie-shape figure with pieces reflecting the percentages. After selection of the data and activation of the Chart Wizard, the option of the pie chart is chosen.

This is illustrated in Panel 4.20, which contains both the data of the joint budget case of Chapter 3 and the resulting pie chart. The items in the first row are used as labels for each individually colored piece. Pie charts are useful only for this particular application.

Panel 4.20 Data and Pie Chart

UofC	MRC	SAIT	SSW
$ 161,630	$ 100,430	$ 82,170	$ 152,375

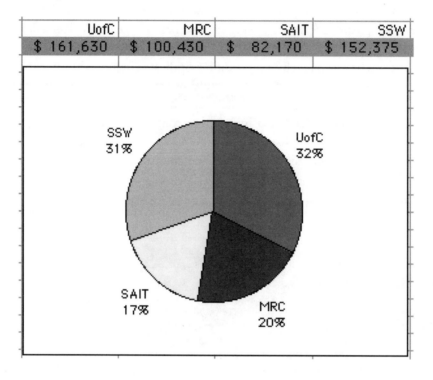

Exercises

4.1 Activate the chart in panel 4.8 supplied on the disk accompanying this book. By means of the *chart, chart type* command change the chart successively into all possible chart types.

Assignments

4.1 Joint Project Charts

Develop a number of suitable charts to illustrate the data and the results of the case treated in Chapter 3.

part 2

Basic Concepts of Financial Economics

Chapter 5
Calculations with Interest Rates

This chapter deals with the fundamentals of financial economics. First the formulas for simple and compound interest are introduced, and corresponding formulas are derived for different compounding periods. Then formulas for the future value of repeated constant payments are explained and derived.

In this chapter you will learn the following spreadsheet commands and functions:

- Workbook level and sheet level names
- FV(*Interest Rate,Term,Amount*)
- Edit Fill

5.1 Simple Interest

On January 1, Year 1, a person buys a five-year Guaranteed Investment Certificate (GIC) for $1,000 or a bond of the same amount, with an interest rate of 8% to be paid out annually. Even for such simple investments, spreadsheets are useful for calculations and displaying results.

The spreadsheet for this investment may be divided into two parts, one for data and one for calculations, see Panel 5.1. The data section contains the main data, which are the amount and the interest rate, A1 and A2, respectively. Cell D1 containing the amount $1,000 is given the name A which is also given in cell C1. Cell D2, which gives the 8% interest rate, is named IR, which is entered in C2. (For some reason R is not a valid name.)

The sheets of the workbook for this chapter contain similar but different data. It is convenient to give the data in each sheet the same names, but this is only possible if the

Panel 5.1 Simple Interest Investment

	A	B	C	D
1	Amount		A	$1,000
2	Interest Rate		IR	8%
3				
4	Year	Cashflow	Principal	Interest
5	1	($1,000)	$1,000	$80
6	2	$80	$1,000	$80
7	3	$80	$1,000	$80
8	4	$80	$1,000	$80
9	5	$80	$1,000	$80
10	6	$1,080		
11				
12	Sum		$400	$400

names only refer to the data of the concerned sheet. In general, names are valid for all sheets of the workbook, which means that they are *workbook level* names. It is also possible to have *sheet level* names which are only valid for the sheet in which they occur. Sheet level names are defined, using the **Insert, Name, Define** command by a name preceded by the sheet name plus exclamation mark.

If cell D1 is to be given the sheet level name A, its name should be entered as PANEL1,2!A, where PANEL1,2 is the name of the first sheet. In formulas of the sheet PANEL1,2, the name A corresponds to cell D2 of that sheet. In other sheets the name A may refer to a sheet level name for that sheet or to a workbook level name.

In the sheets of the workbook for this chapter, all names are at the sheet level. Sheet level names are followed by the sheet name when the command **Insert, Name, Define** displays existing names.

In the calculations in the following the situation at the beginning of each year or period will be presented and the years or periods will be named Year 1, Year 2, and so on. If a different numbering of periods is used, such as 0, 1, and so on, certain formulas may change.

The amounts of money booked on that person's bank account, also called the *cashflow*, at the start of each year, and the principal and interest over the years, are given in the calculations part of the spreadsheet. For the first year the principal, which means the amount over which interest is paid, given by C5, is entered as =A, and the interest in D5 as =IR*C5. The cashflow for the start of Year 2 in cell B6 is then the interest over Year 1, given by =D5. The principal for Year 2 equals that of Year 1, so that C6 contains =C5. The interest in Year 2 is again interest rate times principal, =IR*C6, so that D6 is copied from D5. Then the range B6:D6 is copied to B6:D9. At the start of Year 6, the principal is paid back along with the interest over Year 5, so that B10 contains =C9+D9. Cell B12 contains the sum of the cashflows, =SUM(B5:B10), which is copied to D12 for the sum of interest over the years.

Panel 5.2 gives the cashflow, the principal, and the interest for the six years. This chart is obtained by generating a bar chart from the range A4:D10, using the first row for the legend and the first column for the category values.

In this case interest is paid out immediately after it has been earned. This is called *simple interest*. The total amount of interest received over the five years is 5*80 = $400, which is obtained by summing the cashflow or the interest column.

5.2 Compound Interest

It is also possible that in each year interest is added to the principal, so that it earns interest, and that the only payout is at the start of Year 6. This is called *compound interest* and illustrated in Panel 5.3. In this case the principal for Years 2-5 equals last year's principal plus the interest over that year, so that C6 contains =C5+D5, which is copied downwards. The range B6:B9 is empty, while the rest of the spreadsheet is the same.

Panel 5.2 Cashflow, Principal, and Interest for a 5-Year Bond with Simple Interest

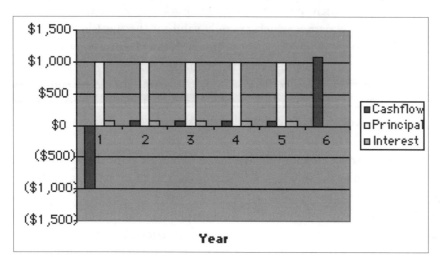

Panel 5.3 Compound Interest Investment

	A	B	C		D
1	Amount			A	$1,000
2	Interest Rate			IR	8%
3					
4		Year	Cashflow	Principal	Interest
5		1	($1,000)	$1,000	$80
6		2		$1,080	$86
7		3		$1,166	$93
8		4		$1,260	$101
9		5		$1,360	$109
10		6	$1,469		
11					
12	Sum		$469		$469

Panel 5.4 gives the cashflow, principal and interest in the bar chart form. There are only two cash flows, one at the beginning and one at the end.

It is obvious that money put on compound interest accumulates faster than on simple interest, because summing the cashflow now results in $469, which is $69 more than for simple interest. Algebraically, it is easily seen that the principal is multiplied every year by the factor $1 + r$, so that, if an amount A is put on compound interest, with an annual interest rate of r, its value after t years will be

$$A(1+r)^t.$$

This formula represents the *future value* of the amount A after t periods of compound interest investment at rate r.

Panel 5.4 Cashflow, Principal, and Interest for 5-Year Bond with Compound Interest

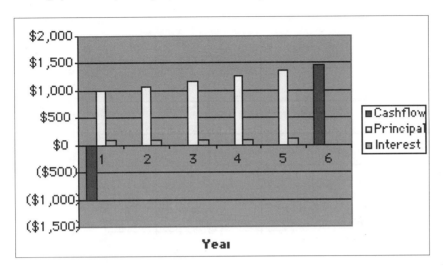

Panel 5.5 Compound Interest Results

	A	B	C	D	E	F
1	Amount	A	$1,000			
2						
3	Years\ Interest	2%	3%	5%	10%	15%
4	1	$1,020	$1,030	$1,050	$1,100	$1,150
5	5	$1,104	$1,159	$1,276	$1,611	$2,011
6	10	$1,219	$1,344	$1,629	$2,594	$4,046
7	15	$1,346	$1,558	$2,079	$4,177	$8,137
8	20	$1,486	$1,806	$2,653	$6,727	$16,367
9	30	$1,811	$2,427	$4,322	$17,449	$66,212

Panel 5.5 gives the future values for A = $1,000, and a number of values for t and r, while Panel 5.6 gives these values in graphical form. Cell B4 contains the formula

$$=A*(1+B\$3)^\wedge\$A4$$

which is copied to B4:F9.

Note the effect of higher interest rates for longer horizons. For $r = 2$–3% it takes 30 years to double the original amount. For $r = 5\%$, it takes 15 years, for $r = 10\%$, 7 years, and for $r = 15\%$, only 5 years.

Long-term interest rates have historically varied from 3% to 15%, and with an average of around 10% over the last 10 years. But the average inflation rate over the last 10 years has been 5%, so that the real interest rate has been around 5%.

Short-term and long-term interest rates may be different. For example, a 1-year GIC may give a 6% interest, a 5-year GIC 7%, while a 10-year government bond may give 8%. The following is based on the interest rate being the same for all terms.

Panel 5.6 The Effect of Compound Interest

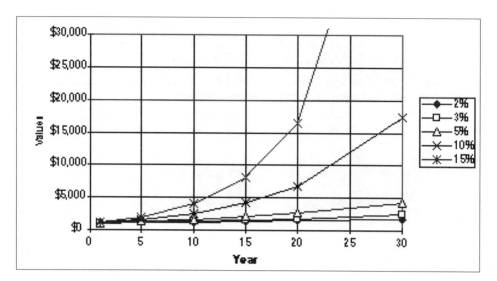

The future value formula is, of course, valid for all kinds of constant percentage growth, such as long-term economic growth expressed in the growth of real Gross Domestic Product (GDP) or income per capita, inflation, population growth, resource use, and environmental degradation, to name just a few. From Panels 5.5 and 5.6 we see that a growth of 2-3% leads to doubling in a generation, 30 years, a growth of 5% results in doubling after 15 years, of 10% after 7 years, and of 15% after 5 years.

5.3 The Effect of Changing the Compounding Period

What will happen if the compounding, instead of every year, is done every half year? If the annual rate of interest is 8%, it must be 4% per half year, but then there will be twice as many periods over which to compound. For the five year example the total amount to be paid out will then be:

$$1,000(1 + \frac{0.08}{2})^{10} = 1,480.24.$$

Since this is more than $1,469, we may wish to compound more often than twice per year. For compounding n times per year, the result is:

$$1,000(1 + \frac{0.08}{n})^{5n}.$$

For example, compounding daily with an annual interest of 8% results in:

$$1,000(1 + \frac{0.08}{365})^{5*365} = 1,491.76.$$

If the initial amount is A, the interest rate is 100r% and the number of years is t, the amount after t years with n times compounding is

Panel 5.7 Returns of $1,000 over 5 Years for Different Compounding Periods

	A	B	C	D	E	F	G	H	I	J	K	L
1	Amount		A $1,000									
2												
3		n	2%	4%	6%	8%	10%	12%	14%	16%	18%	20%
4	Annual	1	$1,104	$1,217	$1,338	$1,469	$1,611	$1,762	$1,925	$2,100	$2,288	$2,488
5	Quarterly	4	$1,105	$1,220	$1,347	$1,486	$1,639	$1,806	$1,990	$2,191	$2,412	$2,653
6	Monthly	12	$1,105	$1,221	$1,349	$1,490	$1,645	$1,817	$2,006	$2,214	$2,443	$2,696
7	Weekly	52	$1,105	$1,221	$1,350	$1,491	$1,648	$1,821	$2,012	$2,223	$2,456	$2,713
8	Daily	365	$1,105	$1,221	$1,350	$1,492	$1,649	$1,822	$2,013	$2,225	$2,459	$2,718
9	Contin.	Inf.	$1,105	$1,221	$1,350	$1,492	$1,649	$1,822	$2,014	$2,226	$2,460	$2,718
10												
11	Inc. Daily/An.		0%	0%	1%	2%	2%	3%	5%	6%	7%	9%

$$A(1 + \frac{r}{n})^{tn}.$$

To find out what happens for n → ∞, the above expression is rewritten with m = n/r:

$$\text{Lim}_{m\rightarrow\infty} A\{(1+\frac{1}{m})^m\}^{rt} = Ae^{rt},$$

where $e = \text{Lim}_{m\rightarrow\infty} A(1+\frac{1}{m})^m = 2.718..$ is the base of natural logarithms.

For A = 1,000, r = 8% and t = 5 years, we find 1491.82.

An overview of the results of compounding for different periods with annual interest rates varying from 2–20% is given in Panel 5.7. Note that different compounding periods result in significantly different results only for higher interest rates. Some banks advertise with savings accounts that are daily compounded. The last row of the table gives the increase in return of daily compounding over annual compounding.

As multiple compounding within a year increases the return, it is equivalent to an increase in the annual interest rate. For an annual interest rate with monthly compounding $r_c(m)$, the return after one year equals 1 + the equivalent annual interest rate with annual compounding, r:

$$(1 + \frac{r_c(12)}{12})^{12} = 1 + r.$$

so that

$$r = (1 + \frac{r_c(12)}{12})^{12} - 1.$$

If the compounding takes place n times per year with an annual interest rate of rc(n) the equivalent interest rate with annual compounding is:

$$r = (1 + \frac{r_c(n)}{n})^n - 1. \tag{1}$$

For continuous compounding with an annual interest rate of rc(•) we have

$$r = e^{r_c(\cdot)} - 1 = EXP(r_c(\cdot)) - 1. \tag{2}$$

Panel 5.8 gives the interest rates equivalent with the annual interest rates with more frequent compounding. The formula for cell C2 is:

=(1+C$1/$B2)^$B2−1

which is copied to C2:L6. Cell C7 contains the formula =EXP(C$1) − 1, which is copied to the right.

Note that for low interest rates, more frequent compounding does not make much difference, but at 10% the difference is about 0.5%, at 14%, 1% and at 20%, 2%.

Panel 5.8 Interest Rates Equivalent with Annual Interest Rates with Compounding

	A	B	C	D	E	F	G	H	I	J	K	L
1		n	2%	4%	6%	8%	10%	12%	14%	16%	18%	20%
2	Annual	1	2.00%	4.00%	6.00%	8.00%	10.00%	12.00%	14.00%	16.00%	18.00%	20.00%
3	Quarterly	4	2.02%	4.06%	6.14%	8.24%	10.38%	12.55%	14.75%	16.99%	19.25%	21.55%
4	Monthly	12	2.02%	4.07%	6.17%	8.30%	10.47%	12.68%	14.93%	17.23%	19.56%	21.94%
5	Weekly	52	2.02%	4.08%	6.18%	8.32%	10.51%	12.73%	15.01%	17.32%	19.68%	22.09%
6	Daily	365	2.02%	4.08%	6.18%	8.33%	10.52%	12.75%	15.02%	17.35%	19.72%	22.13%
7	Contin.	Inf	2.02%	4.08%	6.18%	8.33%	10.52%	12.75%	15.03%	17.35%	19.72%	22.14%

On the other hand, we may wish to know the annual interest rate with compounding n times per year, $r_c(n)$, which is equivalent to an annual interest rate r. Using the equation (1), we have

$$(1 + \frac{r_c(n)}{n})^n = 1 + r.$$

Solving for $r_c(n)$, we find:

$$r_c(n) = n\{(1+r)^{1/n} - 1\}.$$

The equivalent annual compound interest rates are given in Panel 5.9. Cell C2 is based on the formula:

=$B2*((1+C$1)^(1/$B2)−1),

which is copied to C3:L6.

For the infinite case we have from (2):

$$e^{r_c(\cdot)} = 1 + r,$$

so that

$r_c(\cdot) = \ln(1+r)$.

Cell C7 is therefore given the formula:

=LN(1+C$1),

which is copied to the right.

The result is that if compounding takes place more frequently, the annual interest rate on which interest payments are based should be less. For example, if you have a student loan with an simple annual interest rate of 10%, and interest must be paid every month, interest calculations should be based on an annual rate of 9.57% rather than 10%.

Panel 5.9 Equivalent Annual Compound Interest Rates

	A	B	C	D	E	F	G	H	I	J	K	L
1		n	2%	4%	6%	8%	10%	12%	14%	16%	18%	20%
2	Annual	1	2.00%	4.00%	6.00%	8.00%	10.00%	12.00%	14.00%	16.00%	18.00%	20.00%
3	Quarterly	4	1.99%	3.94%	5.87%	7.77%	9.65%	11.49%	13.32%	15.12%	16.90%	18.65%
4	Monthly	12	1.98%	3.93%	5.84%	7.72%	9.57%	11.39%	13.17%	14.93%	16.67%	18.37%
5	Weekly	52	1.98%	3.92%	5.83%	7.70%	9.54%	11.35%	13.12%	14.86%	16.58%	18.26%
6	Daily	365	1.98%	3.92%	5.83%	7.70%	9.53%	11.33%	13.11%	14.85%	16.56%	18.24%
7	Cont	Inf	1.98%	3.92%	5.83%	7.70%	9.53%	11.33%	13.10%	14.84%	16.55%	18.23%

5.4 The Future Value of Repeated Constant Payments

If the same amount of money is being received every year over a number of years, this is called an *annuity*. An annuity may have a fixed term, which means that the amount is paid out for a given number of years, or it may be based on the life of a person, in which case it is paid out for as long as that person lives. Here we shall deal only with fixed-term annuities.

Panel 5.10 gives the pay-outs of a 10-year annuity with an annual amount $10,000. The same values may also represent annual amounts put into a savings account. In both cases, we can ask what the total future value is of the annual amounts at the end of the 10 years if the interest rate is 8%. This future value may be obtained in three ways: (1) explicit spreadsheet calculation, (2) algebraic calculation, (3) spreadsheet formula calculation.

5.4.1 Explicit Spreadsheet Calculation

This future value may be obtained by determining the future value of each annual amount in Year 10, and adding these. This is done in column C of Panel 5.10. Cell C5 contains the formula

=B5*(1+IR)^($A$14–$A5),

which is copied to the range C5:C14. The desired future value is then found as the sum of this range, which is $144,866, where $44,866 is due to accumulated interest.

Panel 5.10 Future Value of an Annuity

	A	B	C
1	Amount	A	$10,000
2	Int Rate	IR	8%
3			
4	Year	Annual Am.	Fut Values
5	1	$10,000	$19,990
6	2	$10,000	$18,509
7	3	$10,000	$17,138
8	4	$10,000	$15,869
9	5	$10,000	$14,693
10	6	$10,000	$13,605
11	7	$10,000	$12,597
12	8	$10,000	$11,664
13	9	$10,000	$10,800
14	10	$10,000	$10,000
15	Sum	$100,000	$144,866

The same scheme may apply to a student loan of a constant annual amount taken over, say, a 4-year period. The future value is then the total amount of the loan when the last amount is received.

The same future value can be used for what is called a *reverse mortgage*. For such a mortgage a contract is made where a property owner, usually of retirement age, receives, for example, $10,000 per year for 10 years from a financial institution. After 10 years the property is sold, and the future value of the annuity is taken out of the sales proceeds. If the interest rate is 8%, the future value of the annuity would be $144,866, as indicated in Panel 5.10. The annual amounts received are in fact loans with the property as security.

5.4.2 Algebraic Calculation
The spreadsheet makes it easy to perform the required calculations, but it is possible to derive a more concise algebraic formula.

Let the annual amount of the annuity be A, its term (number of years) t, and the interest rate r.

After one year the amount will be A, after two years, A + (1+r)A, after three years, A + (1+r)A + (1+r)^2A, and after t years:

$$\{1 + (1+r) + (1+r)^2 + \ldots + (1+r)^{t-1}\}A = (1 + R + R^2 + .. + R^{t-1})A, \tag{3}$$

where $R = 1 + r$. The formula for the summation of a geometric series with ratio R, a first term F, and a last term L, is

$$\frac{F - RL}{1 - R},$$

Panel 5.11 Future Values of Constant Payments

	A	B	C	D	E	F
1	Amount	A	$1,000			
2						
3	Years \ Interest	2%	3%	5%	10%	15%
4	1	$1,000	$1,000	$1,000	$1,000	$1,000
5	5	$5,204	$5,309	$5,526	$6,105	$6,742
6	10	$10,950	$11,464	$12,578	$15,937	$20,304
7	15	$17,293	$18,599	$21,579	$31,772	$47,580
8	20	$24,297	$26,870	$33,066	$57,275	$102,444
9	30	$40,568	$47,575	$66,439	$164,494	$434,745

Panel 5.12 Chart for Future Value of Constant Payments

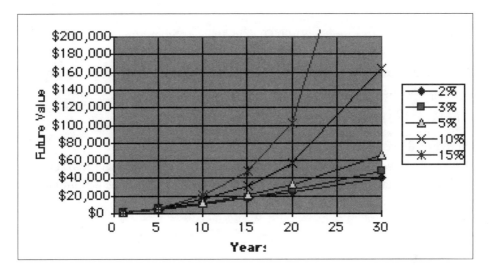

For (3) we find therefore:

$$\frac{1-(R)(R^{t-1})}{1-R} \quad A = \frac{1-R^t}{1-R} \quad A = \frac{R^t-1}{r}A,$$

so that the formula for the future value indicated by P_t is:

$$P_t = \frac{(1+r)^t-1}{r}A = (((1+r)\hat{\ }t-1)/r)*A. \tag{4}$$

5.4.3 Spreadsheet Formula Calculation

Formula (4) is implemented in the spreadsheet function for future value:

=FV(Interest Rate, Term, -Annual Amount) or =FV(r,t,-A).

Note that the annual amount should be entered with a minus-sign, since this can be considered as a payment, leading to a positive cash flow.

In Panel 5.10, cell B4 is given the formula

=FV(B$3,$A4,–A)

which is copied to B4:F9.

Panels 5.11 and 5.12 give the future values of constant payments for years varying from 1–30, and for interest rates varying from 2–15%. With annual savings of $1,000, a total value of $100,000 can be reached in 20 years if the interest rate is 15%, or in 25 years for a rate of 10%.

5.4.4 Annual Payment
How large A should be give a future value Pt? This is found by solving (3) for A:

$$A = \frac{r}{(1+r)^t - 1} \, P_t.$$

For example, to accumulate $1,000,000 in 20 years when the interest rate is 5%, requires annual savings of $30,243.

Panel 5.13 gives, for a future value of $1,000,000 the annual payments required for various interest rates and terms. Cell B5 has the formula

=PT*B$3/((1+B$3)^$A4 – 1)

which is copied to B4:F9.

Panel 5.14 gives the same results in graphical form. For an annual interest rate or yield of 10%, annual savings of about $6,000 are sufficient to become a millionaire in 30 years.

5.5 Spreadsheet Features

5.5.1 The Fill Command
In many cases a spreadsheet contain columns or rows filled with numbers such as 1 2 3 4, or 1994 1995 ... 2019. These can be generated by first entering in the first two cells of the range the appropriate numbers such as 1, 2, and then, after selecting the entire range to be filled in, using the command **Edit, Fill, Series, Auto_Fill**.

Alternatively, the first value in the range may be entered, and then the range selected, after which the **Edit, Fill, Series** command is selected with a step value. The default Type Linear generates an arithmetic series. A geometric series can be generated using the Type Growth.

5.5.2 Creative Copying
Earlier it was shown that many parts of spreadsheets can be copied from other parts, so that large spreadsheets can be created with relatively small effort. But the **Copy** command can also be used in more creative ways, which is explained in the following.

Panel 5.13 Annual Savings Needed to Accumulate One Million Dollars

	A	B	C	D	E	F
1	Amount	PT	$1,000,000			
2						
3	Years \ Interest	2%	3%	5%	10%	15%
4	1	$1,000,000	$1,000,000	$1,000,000	$1,000,000	$1,000,000
5	5	$192,158	$188,355	$180,975	$163,797	$148,316
6	10	$91,327	$87,231	$79,505	$62,745	$49,252
7	15	$57,825	$53,767	$46,342	$31,474	$21,017
8	20	$41,157	$37,216	$30,243	$17,460	$9,761
9	30	$24,650	$21,019	$15,051	$6,079	$2,300

Panel 5.14 Chart for Annual Savings Needed to Become a Millionaire

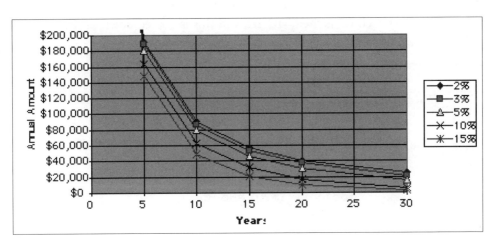

Panel 5.15 Cumulative Sum

	A	B	C	D
1	Item	Amount	Balance	
2			$0	
3	1	$1,000	$1,000	=C2+B3
4	2	($54)	$946	=C3+B4
5	3	($265)	$681	=C4+B5
6	4	($20)	$661	=C5+B6

5.5.2.1 Cumulative Sum

Consider a checking account with an initial balance and a number of items to be added or subtracted, see Panel 5.15.

The balance after each of these items has been entered should be found. This amounts to the *cumulative sum* of the items. Cell C3 should therefore contain =C2+B3, cell C4, =C3+B4, and so on. Instead of entering this separately into each cell, just cell C3 is filled manually, and its content is then copied into C3:C6. Since the spreadsheet uses relative cell addresses when copying, for C4 the content of C3 is translated as =C3+B4, and so on.

If C3 had been empty, the result would have been the same, as empty cells have a numeric value of 0. Cells containing a label also have a numeric value of 0, so that, if row 2 is deleted, the resulting cell C2 has the formula =C1+B2, and displays the value 1,000.

5.5.2.2 First Difference

If the Balance column was known, but the Amount column was not, it may be found in a similar manner. Cell C3 is then =B3-B2, and this is copied downwards, see Panel 5.16. In this way first differences of a series are easily generated.

Panel 5.16 First Difference

	A	B	C	D
1	Item	Balance	Amount	
2		$0		
3	1	$1,000	$1,000	=B3-B2
4	2	$946	($54)	=B4-B3
5	3	$681	($265)	=B5-B4
6	4	$661	($20)	=B6-B5

5.5.2.3 Arithmetic and Geometric Series

Copying with relative cell names can also be used to generate an arithmetic or geometric series. For example, if the factors of compound interest $1, 1+r, (1+r)^2, ..,$ are needed, we enter 1 in A1, =(1+r)*A1 in A2, and then copy A2 downwards, which results in the required geometric series, see Panel 5.17. For an arithmetic series, replace * by +.

Panel 5.17 Geometric Series

	A	B
1	1.00	
2	1.08	=1.08*A1
3	1.17	=1.08*A2
4	1.26	=1.08*A3
5	1.36	=1.08*A4

Exercise

5.1 Suppose a person decides to save every month $100, for a number of years. The interest rate is given as an annual percentage with monthly compounding. Using the future value function, build a table for the value of the savings after 15–25 years, varied by 1, for interest rates of 8–12%, varying by 0.5%.

Assignments

5.1 Study Fund

You have just become the happy parent of a new child. You wish to provide for a study fund of $40,000 by the time the child will be 19 years old by putting a fixed amount into this fund every year, beginning at birth.

(a) How much should you put into this fund every year if the interest rate is 8%?

(b) Find the future value of each annual contribution and the corresponding total value.

(c) Assume that $10,000 is needed at ages 19, 20, 21, and 22. What are the annual amounts?

(d) Assume that an extra $1,000 is provided at birth by another person. What then is the answer to question c?

(e) The above questions imply that it is possible to invest at the same interest rate in each year in a security maturing at the proper time. Is this realistic? If interest rates change over time, how can the goals of the study fund be reached?

(f) How can inflation be taken into account? What will be the answers to question c for real interest rates of 3%, 4%, and 5%?

Chapter 6
Mortgage Loans

This chapter deals with the basics of loans and mortgage loans. Particular attention is paid to mortgage loans, as many people are involved with these. Loans with constant repayments and constant total payments are explained. The formula for constant total payment for loan repayment and interest payment is derived. Amortization periods and terms of mortgage loans are distinguished. Formulas relating interest rates for different compounding periods are used to find monthly mortgage payments.

In this chapter you will learn the following spreadsheet commands and functions

•   PMT (*interest rate, number of periods, principal*)

6.1 Loans with One Repayment

A loan is a contract between a borrower and a lender. The borrower is provided by the lender with an amount of money, which is repaid later, and on which interest is paid. In most cases a fixed rate of interest is agreed to, while also the repayment time schedule must be determined. Depending on the repayment schedule, various forms of loans can be distinguished, namely loans with one repayment, loans with constant periodic repayments, and loans with constant payments for the total of interest and repayment.

A loan can be considered as a fixed interest investment from the viewpoint of the bank or any other party selling the investment. For example, if a bank sells a five-year GIC of $1,000 with an 8% interest rate, it effectively borrows from the buyer $1,000, on which it pays 8% interest, and which it repays after 5 years. Hence it receives at the start of year 1 $1,000, it pays an interest of 8% of $1,000 or $80 in each of the following four years, while it pays in the last year $80 plus the principal of the loan (see Panel 6.1, which is the same as Panel 5.1 of the last chapter, except that all cash flows have the opposite sign). Panel 6.1a gives the number display and Panel 6.1b the formula display.

Panel 6.2 gives a chart of the corresponding cash flow. It indicates that the borrower receives an initial amount, which has to be repaid together with the interest in the following periods. This is the typical pattern of a loan in which just one initial amount is received. Most of the loans discussed in the following are of this type.

The amount borrowed is called the *principal*. The negative cash flows of the following periods consist of interest and repayment of the principal. The repayment is also called the *amortization* of the loan. Amortization can take various forms. The number of periods over which the principal is repaid is called the *amortization period*.

In the above case the entire principal was repaid after 5 years and the interest was paid out in each intermediate and in the last period. Since only the interest is paid to the lender in each year, the principal remains the same, and the interest paid out must

Panel 6.1a The GIC as a Loan (number display)

	A	B	C	D
1	Amount		P	$1,000
2	Interest Rate		IR	8%
3				
4	Year	Cashflow	Principal	Interest
5	1	$1,000	$1,000	$80
6	2	($80)	$1,000	$80
7	3	($80)	$1,000	$80
8	4	($80)	$1,000	$80
9	5	($80)	$1,000	$80
10	6	($1,080)		
11				
12	Sum	($400)		$400

Panel 6.1b The GIC as a Loan (formula display)

	A	B	C	D
1	Amou		P	1000
2	Intere		IR	0.08
3				
4	Year	Cashflow	Principal	Interest
5	1	=P	=P	=IR*C5
6	2	=-D5	=P	=IR*C6
7	3	=-D6	=P	=IR*C7
8	4	=-D7	=P	=IR*C8
9	5	=-D8	=P	=IR*C9
10	6	=-P-D9		
11				
12	Sum	=SUM(B5:B11)		=SUM(D5:D11)

then also be the same for each year.

A special case of this type of loan occurs when the loan is never paid back, which means that the amortization period is infinite. The interest payments are then a stream of infinite duration. Bonds of this sort, called *perpetuals*, were issued by the United Kingdom government at one time. They have since disappeared because they have been bought up by the issuer.

Panel 6.2 Borrower's Cash Flow

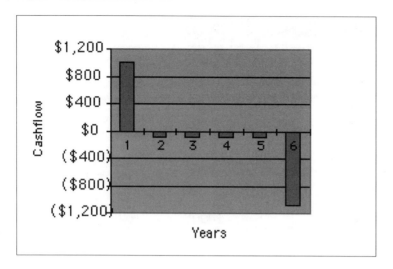

6.2 Loans with Constant Repayments

In the next case to be considered, the repayment is spread over a number of periods. Panels 6.3 and 6.4 illustrate this for the same data as in Panel 6.1. The amortization period is 5 years, and the repayment in each year is therefore 1,000/5 = 200, so that the cells of E6:E10 have the formula

=A/AP.

The principal in Year 2 equals the principal in Year 1 minus the repayment, so that C7 has the formula

=C6–E6.

The interest formula in cell D6 is

=IR*C6.

The cashflow for Year 2 equals (minus) the interest plus repayment related Year 1, so that the formula for B7 is

=–(D6+E6).

These formulas may be copied downwards. This results in a principal of 0 in Year 6, so that the loan has been paid back entirely. Note that the total amount of interest paid is now $240, versus $400 in the previous case, which is explained by the earlier partial repayments.

The constant repayment loan is usually more attractive to the borrower than the one repayment loan, because the repayments are more spread out and therefore smaller, so that they are easier to manage for most people.

Panel 6.3 Loan Amortization with Constant Repayments

	A	B	C	D	E
1	Amount		P	$1,000	
2	Interest Rate		IR	8%	
3	Amortization Period		AP	5	
4					
5		Year Cashflow	Principal	Interest	Repayment
6	1	$1,000	$1,000	$80	$200
7	2	($280)	$800	$64	$200
8	3	($264)	$600	$48	$200
9	4	($248)	$400	$32	$200
10	5	($232)	$200	$16	$200
11	6	($216)	$0		
12					
13	Sum	($240)		$240	$1,000

Panel 6.4 Cash Flow for Loan with Constant Repayments

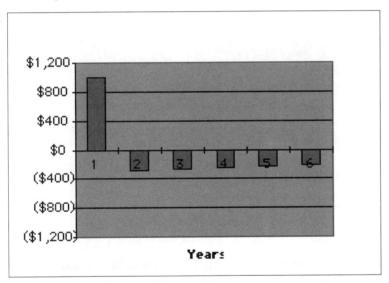

6.3 Loans with Constant Total Payments

Loans with constant repayments have the same repayment in each year, but the interest payments decrease over time, as the principal becomes smaller. In the example of Panel 6.3, interest payments vary from $80 to $16, so that total payments are $280 at the end of Year 1, and $216 at the end of Year 5. It may be more convenient for borrowers to have a repayment scheme such that the total payments, including repayments and interest, are the same for each year. The problem is then to find this constant annual payment. First an algebraic formula will be derived.

Let this constant annual payment be A, the (initial) loan principal P, the amortization period t years, and the interest rate r. The amount owed after t years is according to compound interest:

$$(1+r)^t P.$$

This amount should be equal to the future value of annual payments A during t years,

$$\frac{(1+r)^t-1}{r} A,$$

see formula (3) of the previous chapter. Hence we have the equation:

$$(1+r)^t P = \frac{(1+r)^t-1}{r} A.$$

Substituting $1+r=R$, we may write this as

$$R^t P = \frac{R^t-1}{r} A$$

Solving for A, we find:

$$A = \frac{rR^t}{R^t-1} P = \frac{r}{1-(1+r)^{-t}} P = (r/(1-(1+r)^{-t}))P. \qquad (1)$$

In terms of a spreadsheet formula this may be written as

=P*IR/(1−(1+IR)^−AP)

For the case at hand, we have $P = 1,000, r = 8\%,$ and $t = 5$, so that

$$A = \frac{0.08}{1-(1+0.08)^{-5}} \; 1000 = 250.46.$$

A special spreadsheet function

$$PMT(r,t,-P) = PMT(IR,AP,-P)$$

gives the same result. Note the minus sign in front of the P. This allows A and P to have opposite signs, reflecting that one is a payment and the other a receipt.

6.4 Mortgage Loans

When a real estate property is bought, part of the purchase price is usually financed by a mortgage loan. This is a loan in which the real estate property serves as a security for the repayment of the loan and the payment of the interest. In case of nonpayment the lender has the right to sell the property in order to obtain the amount due.

As an example, consider a mortgage loan with a principal of $50,000 to be paid back, or amortized, in 10 years, so that the *amortization period* is 10 years. For constant repayments, the annual repayment is 50,000/10 = $5,000. The interest rate is 10%.

This interest rate is fixed for the *term* of the mortgage. Here it is assumed that the term is the same as the amortization period, or, what amounts to the same, that the mortgage after a shorter term can be renewed at the same interest rate.

The spreadsheet of Panel 6.5 gives the calculations for this mortgage. Repayments are always $5,000. The principal in any year equals the principal of last year minus the repayment of that year, so that cell B7 has as formula B6–C6, which is copied to B7:B15. The interest equals 10% of the principal so that C6 has as formula B6*IR, which is copied downwards. Finally, total payment equals interest plus repayment.

Panel 6.5a Mortgage Amortization with Constant Repayment (number display)

	A	B	C	D	E
1	Principal		P	$ 50,000	
2	Int Rate		IR	10%	
3	Amort Period		AP	10	
4					
5	Y.	Principal	Repmt	Interest	Tot Pmt
6	1	$50,000	$5,000	$5,000	$10,000
7	2	$45,000	$5,000	$4,500	$9,500
8	3	$40,000	$5,000	$4,000	$9,000
9	4	$35,000	$5,000	$3,500	$8,500
10	5	$30,000	$5,000	$3,000	$8,000
11	6	$25,000	$5,000	$2,500	$7,500
12	7	$20,000	$5,000	$2,000	$7,000
13	8	$15,000	$5,000	$1,500	$6,500
14	9	$10,000	$5,000	$1,000	$6,000
15	10	$5,000	$5,000	$500	$5,500
16	11	$0			

Panel 6.5b Mortgage Amortization with Constant Repayment (formula display)

	A	B	C	D	E
1	Prir		P	50000	
2	Int I		IR	0.1	
3	Am		AP	10	
4					
5	Y.	Principal	Repmt	Interest	Tot Pmt
6	1	=$D$1	=P/AP	=B6*IR	=D6+C6
7	2	=B6-C6	=P/AP	=B7*IR	=D7+C7
8	3	=B7-C7	=P/AP	=B8*IR	=D8+C8
9	4	=B8-C8	=P/AP	=B9*IR	=D9+C9
10	5	=B9-C9	=P/AP	=B10*IR	=D10+C10
11	6	=B10-C10	=P/AP	=B11*IR	=D11+C11
12	7	=B11-C11	=P/AP	=B12*IR	=D12+C12
13	8	=B12-C12	=P/AP	=B13*IR	=D13+C13
14	9	=B13-C13	=P/AP	=B14*IR	=D14+C14
15	10	=B14-C14	=P/AP	=B15*IR	=D15+C15
16	11	=B15-C15			

The disadvantage of this schedule is that the total payments vary from $10,000 in Year 1 to $5,500 in Year 10, see also Panel 6.6. For this reason, the constant total payment scheme is usually more attractive.

Panel 6.6 Mortgage Payments with Constant Repayments

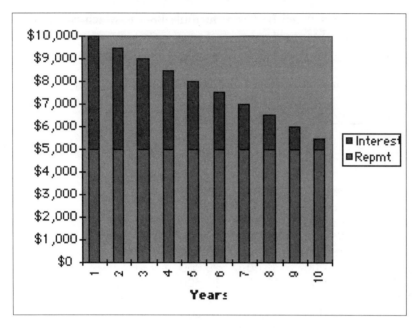

The corresponding mortgage amortization is given in Panel 6.7, see also Panel 6.8.

Panel 6.7 Mortgage Amortization with Constant Total Payments

	A	B	C	D	E
1	Principal		P	$ 50,000	
2	Int Rate		IR	10%	
3	Amort Period		AP	10	
4					
5	Y.	Principal	Repmt	Interest	Tot Pmt
6	1	$50,000	$3,137	$5,000	$8,137
7	2	$46,863	$3,451	$4,686	$8,137
8	3	$43,412	$3,796	$4,341	$8,137
9	4	$39,616	$4,176	$3,962	$8,137
10	5	$35,440	$4,593	$3,544	$8,137
11	6	$30,847	$5,053	$3,085	$8,137
12	7	$25,794	$5,558	$2,579	$8,137
13	8	$20,236	$6,114	$2,024	$8,137
14	9	$14,123	$6,725	$1,412	$8,137
15	10	$7,398	$7,398	$740	$8,137
16	11	$0			

Panel 6.8 Constant Total Payments

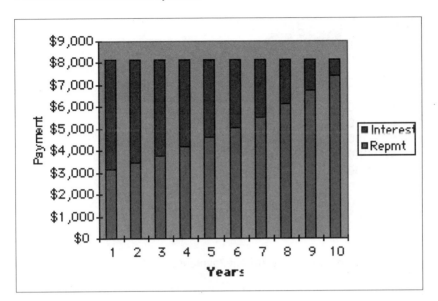

Formula (1) is implemented in the function PMT:

=PMT(*Interest Rate, Term, – Principal*)

For the example we have in E6:E15:

=PMT(IR, AP,– P) = 8,137.

The repayment in D6 is then total payment minus interest which equals E6–C6. After the repayment for Year 10, the principal is 0.

With constant repayments of $5,000 per year the principal of the loan decreases linearly from $50,000 to 0 over the 10 years. This is not true for constant total payments, as in the initial years interest payments are large and repayments small, which is reversed in the last years of the loan. Panels 6.9 and 6.10 give the remaining principal for both types of mortgage finance. Note that it takes 5 years to repay the first $20,000 of the loan. For longer terms and higher interest rates this effect is even stronger.

Note that the sum of interest payments is different for the two schemes: $27,500 for constant repayments versus $31,380 for constant total payments. The reason for this difference is that the latter case the principal is repaid more slowly, so that more interest is due. For both methods the future value of all payments is the same.

Panel 6.9 Remaining Principal for Two Repayment Methods

	A	B	C
1	Year	Const. Rep.	Const. T.P.
2	0	$50,000	$50,000
3	1	$45,000	$46,863
4	2	$40,000	$43,412
5	3	$35,000	$39,616
6	4	$30,000	$35,440
7	5	$25,000	$30,847
8	6	$20,000	$25,794
9	7	$15,000	$20,236
10	8	$10,000	$14,123
11	9	$5,000	$7,398
12	10	$0	$0

Panel 6.10 Unpaid Principal of Loan with Different Payments

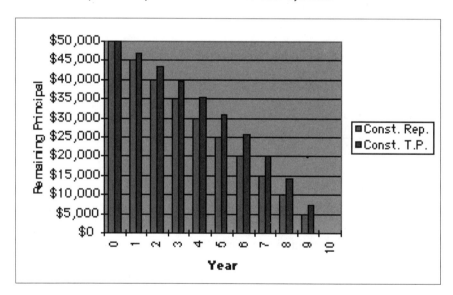

6.5 Monthly Mortgage Payments

Most mortgages on homes are paid on a monthly basis, so that monthly payments are required. These could be approximated by dividing the annual payment by 12: 8,137/12 = $678.11. However, if these amounts are paid in advance of the annual payment, the homeowner loses interest on the amounts prepaid.

We may therefore proceed to use monthly periods so that the interest rate is $^{10}/_{12}$% and the number of periods 12*10. Using the formula for payments (4) or the spreadsheet function we find

$$=PMT(0.1/12, 12*10, -50000) = \$660.75.$$

But this amounts to compounding 12 times per year at an annual interest rate of 10%, which is more costly. What is wanted is the annual interest rate with monthly compounding that is equivalent to annual compounding at 10%. If the desired interest rate is $r_c(m)$, then $r_c(m)$ is determined, as explained earlier, by:

$$r_c(m) = 12((1+0.10)^{1/12} - 1),$$

so that the corresponding monthly interest rate is

$$\frac{r_c(m)}{12} = (1+0.10)^{1/12} - 1 = 0.0080.$$

This may be substituted in the payment function (4) or in the spreadsheet function:

$$=PMT(1.1^{\wedge}(1/12) - 1, 12*10, -50000) = \$648.88.$$

This is 4.5% lower than the first approximation.

In certain cases the mortgage interest rate quoted is based on half-year payments. In such cases this rate must first be converted to the corresponding annual rate using the formula

$$r_a = (1 + r_b/2)^2 - 1,$$

where r_a is the annual and r_b is the half-year rate (expressed as a full year rate). For 10% we obtain:

$$r_a = 1.05^2 - 1 = 10.25\%.$$

The corresponding monthly payments are then

$$=PMT(1.1025^{\wedge}(1/12) - 1, 10*12, -P) = \$655.17,$$

which is nearly 1% higher than the $648.88 found for the annual rate of 10%.

6.6 The Term of a Mortgage Loan

The term of a mortgage loan is the period for which the interest rate is negotiated. The term can be equal to the amortization period, but is usually shorter. Whereas amortization periods can be as long as 25 years, the term can in most cases not exceed 10 years.

The term of a mortgage is important because the interest rate may change during the term, so that, when the interest rate is negotiated for another term, the monthly payments change.

Interest rates differ for different terms. Panel 6.11 gives the rates for terms varying from six months to 10 years at one point of time. For 10 years the rate is about 50% higher than for six months.

Panel 6.11 Interest Rates for Different Terms

	A	B
1	Term, Yrs	Interest
2	0.5	6.125%
3	1	6.500%
4	2	7.250%
5	3	8.000%
6	4	8.250%
7	5	8.500%
8	7	9.000%
9	10	9.500%

Panel 6.12 gives a graphical display using an XY or scatter graph. The selection of a longer term gives protection against further increases in interest rates, while a shorter term allows taking advantage of lower rates.

Panel 6.12 Interest Rates and Terms of Mortgage Loans

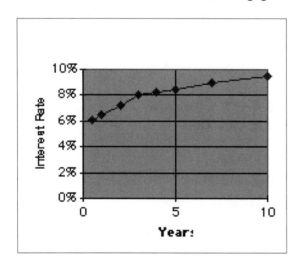

Panels 6.13 and 6.14 illustrate this for a case in which the principal is $100,000 and the amortization period 25 years. It is assumed that interest rates are quoted for bi-annual compounding, but expressed in terms of annual percentages. If the bi-annual rates vary from 5% to 15%, the corresponding annual rates vary from 5.06% to 15.56%, see B7:B17, where B7 has the formula

$$=(1+A7/2)^2-1.$$

The monthly payments in column C are then obtained using as formula for C7:

$$=PMT((1+B7)^{\wedge}(1/12)-1,AP*12,-P).$$

Panel 6.13 Monthly Payments for Varying Interest Rates

	A	B	C
1	Principal	P	$ 100,000
2	Int Rate	IR	10%
3	Amort Period	AP	25
4			
5			
6	Bi-An.Rate	Ann. Rate	M. Payments
7	5.0%	5.06%	$581.60
8	6.0%	6.09%	$639.81
9	7.0%	7.12%	$700.42
10	8.0%	8.16%	$763.21
11	9.0%	9.20%	$827.98
12	10.0%	10.25%	$894.49
13	11.0%	11.30%	$962.53
14	12.0%	12.36%	$1,031.90
15	13.0%	13.42%	$1,102.41
16	14.0%	14.49%	$1,173.88
17	15.0%	15.56%	$1,246.15

It is then observed that monthly payments vary strongly with the interest rate. A mortgage loan that is easily affordable at an interest rate of 6% with monthly payments of $640 may be out of reach at 12% with monthly payments of $1,032. A 1% increase in interest causes monthly payments to go up by $60–70. Usually, the term will be chosen based on the ability to pay the monthly payments and the expectations regarding future interest rates.

For shorter amortization periods, monthly payments will be less sensitive to the interest rate, because the repayment part of the total payment will be larger and the interest part smaller.

Panel 6.14 Relation between Monthly Payments and Interest Rate

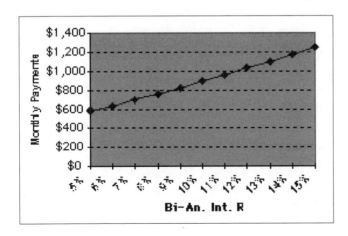

Exercises

6.1 Create a table of monthly payments for bi-annual interest rates varying from 6% to 12% and the principal varying from $60,000–$120,000, assuming the amortization period is 20 years.

6.2 Create a table of monthly payments for bi-annual interest rates varying from 6% to 12% and amortization periods varying from 15–25 years, assuming the principal is $100,000.

6.3 Create a table of monthly payments for the principal varying from $60,000–$120,000, and amortization periods varying from 15–25 years, assuming the bi-annual interest rate is 7%.

6.4 Find for the case of Panel 6.7 the weekly and bi-weekly payments.

6.5 For a monthly payment of $1,000 and an interest rate of 7%, what combinations of principal and amortization period can be afforded?

6.6 Find the monthly payments for the interest rates of Panel 6.5, a principal of $100,000 and an amortization period of 25 years.

6.7 For a monthly payment of $1,000, an amortization period of 25 years, and the interest rates of the terms in Panel 6.7, which amounts of the principal can be afforded?

Assignments

6.1. Mortgage Finance

A couple is considering buying a house with a mortgage loan of $100,000 and a term of 20 years. The mortgage interest rate is currently 8.75%. The mortgage is paid back using a constant annual amount for interest and repayment.

(a) Make up the annual mortgage repayment scheme consisting of principal, interest, repayment and total payment for the 20 years. Use a data section with range names for the data. The scheme should be well designed, with appropriate formats and protection.

(b) Print the mortgage repayment scheme.

(c) (i) What is the future value of the annual total payments after 20 years?

(ii) If monthly instead of annual payments are made, what is the equivalent monthly payment?

(iii) For an annual interest rate of 8.75%, what mortgage loan can be obtained with constant annual total payments of $12,000 over 20 years?

(iv) What mortgage loan for monthly payments of $1,000?

(v) For what interest rate has a loan of $100,000 a monthly payment of $1,000 over 20 years?

(d) Assume now that the interest rate varies every five years, and that in the four five-year periods it is 8.75%, 11.75%, 9.25%, and 7.50%. Payments in the first years are made as if the interest rate will be 8.75% during the 20 years, in the second five years as if the interest rate will be 11.75% in the remaining 15 years, and so on. Make up the resulting annual mortgage repayment scheme, using an extended data section.

(e) Modify this scheme by implementing, using IF, that total annual payments may not exceed a maximum of $12,000 in any year. Use a named cell for this maximum. For what maximum can the mortgage be just paid off in 20 years?

6.2 House Purchase Case

A couple considers buying a home at $100,000, which will be financed by $50,000 of their own capital and a $50,000 mortgage. The mortgage interest is 10% per year with a constant annual payment for interest and principal repayment. The amortization period is 25 years.

(a) Set up a spreadsheet indicating for each year the outstanding principal, the interest due, the principal repayment, and the constant annual repayment. Use a special data section for the data, which should have range names. Print the spreadsheet.

(b) Assume that the property appreciates 5% per year. Determine over the 25 years the value of the home, and the equity in the home (value of the house minus outstanding principal).

(c) Assume that taxes and maintenance costs this year are $3,000 and that in the following years these costs increase by 3% per year. Assume also that the house will be sold in 2016 for the value it has at that time. What is the future value after 25 years of the total costs of the 25 years use of the house? Any costs incurred in earlier years should be compounded to the year the house is sold at an interest rate of 10%.

(d) Instead of owning a house over 25 years, one may be rented at $12,000 per year, with the rent increasing at 6% per year. What is the future value after 25 years of the total costs of 25 years' renting? How does this compare with owning a house?

Chapter 7
Present Values of Periodic Amounts

This chapter introduces discounting and present value applied to constant amounts that are paid out over time, and related to applications. First the concepts of discounting and present value are explained. Then formulas for the present value of annual allowances and other annuities are derived. An overview is given of the various situations, contracts, and formulas that exist related to constant cash flows. Finally, an application to retirement pensions is treated.

In this chapter you will learn the following spreadsheet commands and functions:

- PV(*Interest Rate, Term, Payment*)

7.1 Discounting and Present Value

Suppose that the opportunity exists to purchase an item that in one year's time can be sold for $1,000. How much would one be prepared to pay for it now? This question can be answered if it is known how much we are prepared to pay now for $1 to be received next year. Suppose that currently money is being put into a savings account yielding r% per year. This means that $1 paid now returns $1 + r$ (where r is written per unit, so that 5% is 0.05) one year later. Hence, dividing by $1+r$, we have that $\$1/(1+r)$ now is equivalent to $1 one year later. From this it may be concluded that $\$1,000/(1+r)$ now is equivalent with $1,000 one year later.

If the best alternative use of money is a savings account with $100r$% interest, the opportunity costs of $1 now is $1+r$ in terms of money next year. If X is the amount of dollars now that we are prepared to pay for $1,000 next year, we have for this amount:

$$X(1+r) = 1,000,$$

so that

$$X = \frac{1000}{1+r}.$$

X is defined as the *present value* of 1000. For $r = 0.1$, $X = 1000/(1.1) = 909.09$. The $1,000 is *discounted* to 909.09 by multiplication of the *discount factor*

$$\frac{1}{1+r} = 0.90909.$$

If $1,000 is expected in two years, its present value is the amount, when put on compound interest, results in $1,000 in two years:

$$X(1+r)^2 = 1,000,$$

86

so that

$$X = \frac{1000}{(1+r)^2}.$$

For two years the discount factor is $1/(1.1)^2 = 0.826$.

In general, the present value of an amount of money A available after t years, for an interest rate r is:

$$\frac{A}{(1+r)^t}.$$

Discounting or taking the present value is obviously the inverse process of compound interest. Panel 7.1 displays the present value of $1,000 for varying interest rates and for a varying number of years. C1 is named A and B4 has the formula A/(1+$A4)^B$3, which is copied to B4:O9. Panel 7.2 displays the same information in graphical form.

Of great and practical interest is the rapid decline for increasing t when the interest rates are larger than, say, 5%. A low present value means that the amount of $1,000 is less important. With interest rates of more than 10%, future amounts in 20 years become insignificant.

Panel 7.1 Present Value of $1,000 for Varying Interest Rates and Years

	A	B	C	D	E	F	G	H	I	J	K	L	M	N	O
1	Amount		A	1000											
2															
3	IR\Yr	1	2	3	4	5	6	7	8	9	10	15	20	25	30
4	2%	980	961	942	924	906	888	871	853	837	820	743	673	610	552
5	5%	952	907	864	823	784	746	711	677	645	614	481	377	295	231
6	10%	909	826	751	683	621	564	513	467	424	386	239	149	92	57
7	12%	893	797	712	636	567	507	452	404	361	322	183	104	59	33
8	15%	867	751	651	564	489	423	367	318	276	239	117	57	28	14
9	20%	833	694	579	482	402	335	279	233	194	162	65	26	10	4

Panel 7.2 displays the same results in graphical form. For an interest rate of 10% or higher, amounts in Year 7 or later are more than halved, and dwindle into insignificance. Discounting with higher interest rates amounts to a myopic view, so that only the very near future matters. Only at rates of interest of 2% do time spans like generations, which are about 30 years, matter.

Note that it was assumed implicitly that the interest rate was the same for all years. In a number of cases this may not be valid, especially if both cash flows in the first few years and 10 or 20 years later are involved, as interest rates of government debt of different duration vary.

Panel 7.2 The Present Value of $1,000

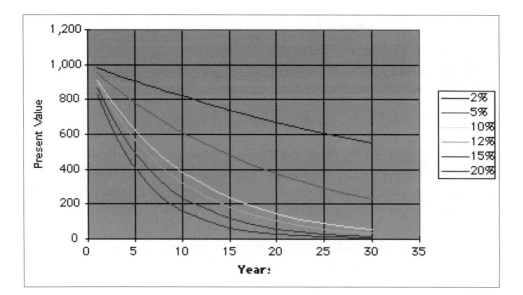

7.2 The Present Value of Study Allowances and Annuities

Suppose one is to receive a study allowance of $10,000 per year for each of the next 10 years. How much is this worth now if the interest rate for discounting purposes is 5%? A series of equal payments over a number of years is called an *annuity*, and the number of years of payments the *term* of the annuity. Sometimes an annuity is only paid out as long as a person is alive, but we shall not consider such annuities here.

First a spreadsheet representation of this problem is presented, then an algebraic treatment,and finally the related spreadsheet function.

Panel 7.3 gives the cash flow of the 10-year annuity, both in number display and formula display, see also Panel 7.4. Each of the amounts may be discounted back to year 0, which is done by dividing the amount in year t by $(1+r)^t$. Cell C5 has as formula =B5/(1+IR)^A5, which is copied downwards. The resulting sum is is $77,217, which is the present value of the ten payments.

It is more convenient to use an algebraic formula, which is derived as follows. Let the amount of the payments be A, the interest rate r, and the term t.

The present value of $1 to be paid out in Year 1 is

$$d = \frac{1}{1+r},$$

and that of $1 to be paid out in year t, d^t.

Hence the total present value P_0 of an amount A paid out every year for t years is

$$P_0 = (d + d^2 + .. + d^t)A = \frac{d(1-d^t)}{1-d} A = \frac{(1-d^t)}{r} A. \tag{1}$$

Panel 7.3a The Present Value of an Annual Allowance (number display)

	A	B	C
1	Amount	A	$ 10,000
2	Int. Rate	IR	5%
3			
4	Year	Cashflow	Disc. Cashfl.
5	0	$0	$0
6	1	$10,000	$9,524
7	2	$10,000	$9,070
8	3	$10,000	$8,638
9	4	$10,000	$8,227
10	5	$10,000	$7,835
11	6	$10,000	$7,462
12	7	$10,000	$7,107
13	8	$10,000	$6,768
14	9	$10,000	$6,446
15	10	$10,000	$6,139
16	Sum	$100,000	$77,217

Panel 7.3b The Present Value of an Annual Allowance (formula display)

	A	B	C
1	Amount	A	10000
2	Int. Rate	IR	0.05
3			
4	Year	Cashflow	Disc. Cashfl.
5	0	0	=B5/(1+IR)^A5
6	1	=A	=B6/(1+IR)^A6
7	2	=A	=B7/(1+IR)^A7
8	3	=A	=B8/(1+IR)^A8
9	4	=A	=B9/(1+IR)^A9
10	5	=A	=B10/(1+IR)^A10
11	6	=A	=B11/(1+IR)^A11
12	7	=A	=B12/(1+IR)^A12
13	8	=A	=B13/(1+IR)^A13
14	9	=A	=B14/(1+IR)^A14
15	10	=A	=B15/(1+IR)^A15
16	Sum	=SUM(B5:B15)	=SUM(C5:C15)

Panel 7.4 Undiscounted and Discounted Cash Flow for an Annuity

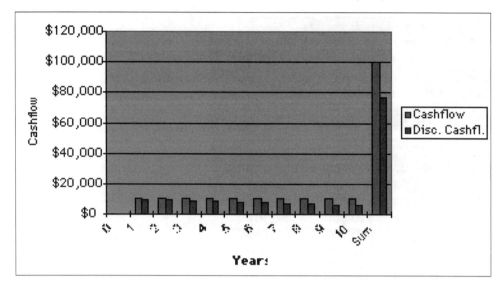

The expression after the second equality is obtained using the geometric series formula.

For $A = 10,000$, $r = 5\%$, and 10 years we find $P_0 = \$77,217$.

For the term of the annuity $t \to \infty$ we find for the annuity present value:

$$P_0 = \frac{A}{r} = \$100,000.$$

This formula is valid for so-called perpetual bonds that are never redeemed, but continue to pay the same rate of interest.

Formula (1) is related to formula (4) of the previous chapter:

$$A = \frac{r}{1-(1+r)^{-t}} P_0.$$

The relationship between P and A is the same, except that it is solved for the present value P_0 in (1), and for A in (4).

Formula (1) is implemented in the spreadsheet function PV which has three arguments:

PV(*Interest, Term, -Amount*).

For our example we have:

$PV(r,t,-A) = PV(10\%,10,-10000) = \$77,217.$

Annuities are usually sold to individuals by banks or other financial institutions with as price the present value as given in (1). Fixed-term annuities are for banks similar to GIC's except that different durations are involved.

Panel 7.5 Calculation of a Bond Return

	A	B	C	D	E
1	Amount	A	$1,000	PV Interest Payments	$406
2	Int. Rate	IR	5%	PV Rep. Principal	$676
3	Price	P	$1,075	Price	($1,075)
4	Disc. IR	DIR	4%	Sum	$6
5					
6	Year	Cashflow	Disc. CF		
7	0	($1,075)	($1,075)		
8	1	$50	$48		
9	2	$50	$46		
10	3	$50	$44		
11	4	$50	$43		
12	5	$50	$41		
13	6	$50	$40		
14	7	$50	$38		
15	8	$50	$37		
16	9	$50	$35		
17	10	$1,050	$709		
18					
19	Sum	$425	$6		
20					
21					

Panel 7.6 Cash Flow for $1,000 Bond

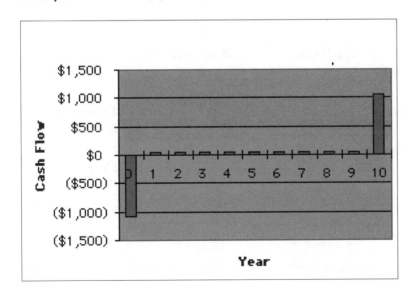

The same formulas can be used to evaluate the return of bonds. Suppose that a $1,000 bond can be bought for $1,075. It yields an annual interest of 5 % and it is going to be paid back after 10 years. Is this an attractive proposition if the bank offers a savings account with an annual interest of 4%? To find this out, the purchase price of $1,075 at the beginning must be compared with the revenues in later years. This can be done using the concept of *present value*, as will be explained below. The bond investment has a certain *cash flow*, which means the outflows and inflows of money related to it. The cash flow for the bond investment is given in Panel 7.5 and illustrated in Panel 7.6.

The problem of the evaluation of the $1,000 bond can be solved in the same way as that of finding the annuity value. Firstly, the cash flows of the successive years can be discounted back to the beginning, after which these are summed together with the purchase price. This is done in column C of Panel 7.5. The resulting sum of the discounted cash flows is $6, so that buying the bond at $1,075 gives a $6 return using a 4% interest rate for discount purposes.

The discounted value of the constant interest payments of $50 during 10 years can be determined by means of the PV formula:

=PV(DIR,10,–IR*A)

which results in $406, see cell E1 in Panel 7.5.

The repayment of the principal can be discounted back to the beginning using the formula:

=1000(1+r)^10 = A/(1+DIR)^10 = $676, see E2.

After subtraction of the purchase price of $1,075, the same return of $6 is found.

7.3 Overview of Constant Cash Flows, and Related Formulas and Contracts

As constant cash flows and their equivalent present and future values have been discussed in a number of contexts, it is useful to give an overview and comparison.

As an example cash flows of $10,000 occurring in Years 1 to 10 will be taken. The interest rate is 10%. The cash flows may be inflows (positive) or outflows (negative), see Panel 7.7. The present value of this cash flow, which is the value in Year 0, is

$$P_0 = \frac{1-(1+r)^{-t}}{r} \; A = PV(r,t,-A) = PV(10\%, 10,-10000) = \$77,217. \tag{2}$$

The future value of the cash flow, which is the value in Year 10 is:

$$P_{10} = \frac{(1+r)^t - 1}{r} \; A = FV(r,t,-A) = FV(10\%, 10,-10000) = \$125,779. \tag{3}$$

An *annuity* is a contract of a person with a financial institution according to which this person pays a sum of money P_0 in year 0 to have cash inflows of A during *t* years. The financial institution sets the interest rate r according to which P_0 is determined. The cash inflows and outflows for the person are then as set out in the left part of Panel 7.7 and part (a) of Panel 7.8. For the financial institution the inflows and outflows are reversed. The combined present value of inflows and outflows, evaluated at the interest rate $r = 5\%$, is exactly 0, as the price of the annuity equals the present value of the constant annual inflows. The same is true for the three other types of contracts.

A *mortgage with constant total payments* is a contract according to which a person obtains from a financial institution the principal P_0 in year 0 and makes payments of A during the *t* following years. P_0 and A are related as in (2), but for a mortgage usually P_0 is first determined, from which then A is found using the PMT function. For the values of A, r, and *t* of $10,000, 10% and 10 years the cash flows for the person are as indicated in the mortgage columns of Panel 7.7 and in part (b) of Panel 7.8.

From Panel 7.7 and parts (a) and (b) of Panel 7.8 it is noted that the cash flows for the mortgage are precisely the reverse of those for the annuity. If a person wanting to buy an annuity and a person needing a mortgage loan could agree on the amount A, the term t, and the interest rate r, they do not need a financial institution.

The future value gives the equivalent of a constant amount cash flow at the end of the *t* years. Both the reverse mortgage and the savings contract use this equivalence. In the *reverse mortgage* a person receives an amount A during *t* years, but must pay back the equivalent amount at the end, see the corresponding columns of Panel 7.7 and part (c) of Panel 7.8.

Panel 7.7 Cash Flows for Four Types of Contract

	A	B	C	D	E	F	G	H	I
1	Amount		A	$10,000					
2	Int. Rate		IR	5%					
3	Term		T	10					
4									
5	Yea	Annuity		Mortgage		Reverse Mortgage		Savings Contract	
6		Inflows	Outflows	Inflows	Outflows	Inflows	Outflows	Inflows	Outflows
7	0		($77,217)	$77,217					
8	1	$10,000				($10,000)	$10,000		($10,000)
9	2	$10,000				($10,000)	$10,000		($10,000)
10	3	$10,000				($10,000)	$10,000		($10,000)
11	4	$10,000				($10,000)	$10,000		($10,000)
12	5	$10,000				($10,000)	$10,000		($10,000)
13	6	$10,000				($10,000)	$10,000		($10,000)
14	7	$10,000				($10,000)	$10,000		($10,000)
15	8	$10,000				($10,000)	$10,000		($10,000)
16	9	$10,000				($10,000)	$10,000		($10,000)
17	10	$10,000				($10,000)	$10,000	($125,779)	$125,779	($10,000)

Panel 7.8 Cash Flows for Four Contract Types

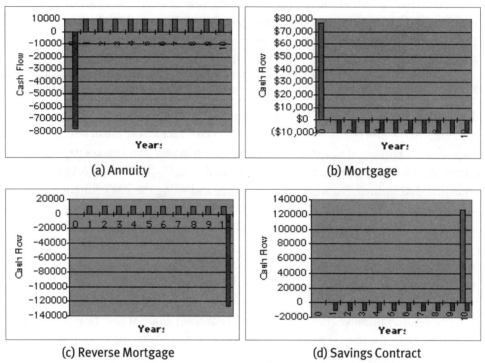

(a) Annuity

(b) Mortgage

(c) Reverse Mortgage

(d) Savings Contract

For a *savings contract*, a person pays an amount A during *t* years, and receives the equivalent amount P_t after *t* years, see the last columns of Panel 7.7 and part (d) of Panel 7.8. Inflows and outflows are the reverse of those of the reverse mortgage.

Two kinds of symmetry can be distinguished in these contracts. Changing from an annuity to a mortgage and vice versa involves changing the sign of all cash flows. The same is true for reverse mortgage and savings contract. Changing from an annuity to a reverse mortgage and vice versa changes the positions of the constant amounts A and their capitalized equivalent given by P_0 or P_t. The same is true for the mortgage and the savings contract. In the annuity one pays in a lump sum for the stream of cash inflows before it is received, so that it is an investment , and in the reverse mortgage after the stream has been received so that it is a loan. In a mortgage loan we receive the money first and then pay it back with a stream of constant amounts, in a savings contract we pay a stream of constant amounts first, and receive its total value in a lump sum at the end.

7.4 Retirement Pensions

The concepts and formulas for periodic payments can be applied to the determination of retirement pensions. In the following setting up retirement provisions for a standard case is considered.

Assume that a person works for 40 years, starting at age 25 and retiring at age 65. The initial salary is $25,000 which increases by 3% per year, until age 55, after which it remains constant. Twelve percent of the salary is saved annually in a pension fund where it accumulates with an interest rate of 5%. The pension fund is used to provide a constant annual pension for 20 years. Required are the annual amount of the pension and the equivalent monthly pension.

Panel 7.9 gives a part of the spreadsheet for the calculations. The data are entered in the usual fashion with appropriate names.

Panel 7.9 Data and Pension Fund Contributions

	A	B	C	D
1	DATA			
2	Starting Salary		SS	$25,000
3	Salary Increment		SI	3%
4	Pension Contribution		PC	12%
5	Interest Rate		IR	5%
6				
7	Age	Salary	P.Contr.	Acc.P.F.
8	25	$25,000	$3,000	$3,000
9	26	$25,750	$3,090	$6,240

It is possible to derive comprehensive algebraic formulas for salaries, contributions to the pension fund, and the pension itself. However, the resulting formulas are complicated, and it is easy to make mistakes. It is preferable to enter for each year, from age 25–84, the various amounts which are easily determined. Moreover, such an annual display makes the entire scheme easier to understand.

First the salaries over the working life must be determined. Cell B8 contains as formula =SS, and cell B9, =B8*(1+SI), which is copied downwards to age 55. The salaries up to age 64 are then made equal to those at 55 by the formula =$B$38.

The pension contribution for each year equals 12% of the salary for that year, so that cell C8 contains as formula =SI*B8, which is copied downwards. The accumulated pension fund amount for a certain year equals that of last year, plus the interest, plus the contribution for the current year, so that cell D8 is given the formula =C8+(1+IR)*D7, which is copied downwards.

The result is an amount of $554,525 at the end of age 64, see Panel 7.10. On this amount the pension, which is to last for 20 years, must be based. It is derived using the formula

=PMT(IR,20,–$D$47)

in cell E84, which is copied downwards. To check whether the funds are exhausted after age 84, cell D84 is given the formula =(1+IR)*D47–E48, which is copied downwards, and which is found to be indeed 0 in cell D67.

Panel 7.10 Switch to Pension

	A	B	C	D	E
7	Age	Salary	P.Contr.	Acc.P.F.	Pension
46	63	$60,682	$7,282	$521,184	
47	64	$60,682	$7,282	$554,525	
48	65			$537,754	$44,496
49	66			$520,146	$44,496

As pensions are usually paid out monthly, rather than annually, the monthly pension should be found, which is done using the formula

$=$PMT$((1+$IR$)^{}(1/12)-1,12*20,-$D$47) = \$3,626.$

Note that the equivalent monthly interest rate is used.

Panel 7.11 gives these pension results. It also indicates that the annual pension is 73% of the last salary. In a number of cases, the pension entitlements are indicated as a percentage of the last salary per year worked. For the case at hand, this amounts to 1.83%.

Panel 7.11 Pension Results

	E	F	G
1	RESULTS		
2	Annual		$44,496
3	Monthly		$3,626
4	% of Last Sal.		73%
5	% of LS/Years Worked		1.83%

Panel 7.12 contains a chart for the accumulated pension fund from the start of work at age 25 to the depletion of the fund at age 84. The fund first accumulates slowly, but increases rapidly at the end of the work life. The same is true for the pension phase, where the decline starts slowly, but is more rapid towards the end.

Panel 7.12 The Accumulated Pension Fund over Work and Retirement Phases

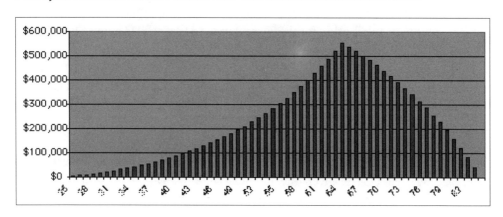

A similar chart can be made for the pension related cash flow for the person concerned, see Panel 7.13. Due to compound interest, a saving of a relatively small amount per year during 40 working years results in a reasonable income in the 20 years of retirement.

Panel 7.13 Pension Related Cash Flow

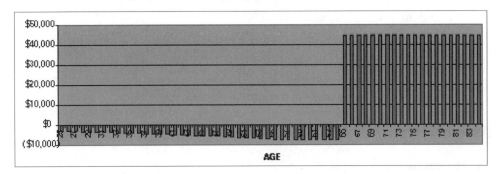

Exercises

7.1 At an interest rate of 7%, what is the present value of a bond yielding 10% to be paid annually, and which will be paid off on December 31, 1999?

7.2 The pension entitlement is the annual pension amount expressed as a percentage of the last salary per year of service. What is the pension entitlement in this case? Calculate the pension entitlement for pension contributions of 10%, 12% and 14% and interest rates of 3%, 4% and 5%.

7.3 In the retirement pension case assume that there is always 4% inflation, and that the salary increase and interest rate given represented only the real increases. Modify the spreadsheet accordingly. What is now the entitlement percentage? Also consider the adjustment of the annual pension amount.

Assignments

7.1 Student Loan Repayment

A student owes a student loan of $20,000. Repayment and payment of interest started on December 1, Year 1 by means of 114 equal monthly payments. The annual interest rate is 10 1/8% with daily compounding.

(a) What is the equivalent annual interest rate with annual compounding?

(b) What are the monthly payments?

(c) Use a table of payments over the 114 months to determine how much is owed on September 1, Year 6 after the monthly payment has been made.

(d) Develop a general formula for the amount owed after t months.

(e) If the remaining principal is repaid in September Year 6, and a corresponding mortgage is taken out at 8.75%, what is the present value of the savings using the mortgage interest rate for discount purposes?

(f) If the remaining principal is repaid in September Year 6 using money that would otherwise have be invested with a return of 6%, what is the present value of the savings using the investment interest rate for discount purposes? Answer the same question if investment returns are taxed at 50%.

part 3

Project Evaluation

Chapter 8
Basic Concepts of Project Evaluation

This chapter introduces project evaluation using discounting and net present value. After some general remarks on investment, the concept of the net present value of an investment project is defined and explained, which is then applied to an example. The appropriate interest rate for discounting purposes is discussed. Finally, the internal rate of return of a project is introduced.

In this chapter you will learn the following spreadsheet commands and functions

* NPV(*interest rate, range*)
* IRR(*range, guess*)

8.1 Introduction

The bond investment of the last chapter is a simple example of a *financial investment*. Such investments typically start with a cash outflow, representing the purchase price of the security. Usually this purchase price is known or is under the control of the decision maker. For bonds and other debt securities the revenues are usually also known, if at least the bonds are considered to be safe. For *equity investments*, such as in shares of a company, the revenues are by no means certain, especially not the value when the investment is sold, so that it is difficult to determine the cash flow.

We may also consider *real investments*, such as buying or building a hotel and running it for a number of years, developing land, setting up a business, and so on. In all these cases the first and major task is the *planning* of the entire enterprise. As a result of this, cash flows can be estimated, and these can be used to determine whether the investment project is profitable and attractive. Spreadsheets are a useful tool for the evaluation of these cash flows.

Governments proceed with investment projects, such as training programs, regional development programs and dams. They usually pay all or most of the investment costs but the revenues go towards certain groups or the population at large. Those benefits, however, can be measured and compared with the costs, irrespective of who pays the costs and who receives the benefits, so that the flows of costs and benefits can be used to find out whether the project is a useful one. This is called *cost-benefit analysis* and spreadsheets provide a convenient environment for studies of this kind.

In the following it is assumed that valid estimates for cash flows or costs and benefits of the project are available. Only in the case of debt investments are cash flows easy to determine, though even in these cases the possibility of default makes it possible to challenge any estimate. Cash flows for shares are of course much more uncertain. Real investment projects, such as setting up a business, usually require enormous amounts of planning and organization, which are not dealt with here. For government projects costs and benefits are even harder to estimate than cash flows.

Unless otherwise stated, it is simply assumed that the difficult task of estimating expected cash flows, and everything related to that, has been performed, and that the results are available.

8.2 The Net Present Value of a Cash Flow

In typical business situations decisions must be made whether a certain project should be undertaken or not. Such a project usually involves expenditures at the start, while revenues come later. To find out whether a project is worthwhile, all revenues and expenditures must be made comparable, which is done by taking their present value.

Assume that a project starts in Year 0, that A_0 is the expenditure (negative) or revenue (positive) connected with the project at that time, that A_1 is the first cash flow of the project in Year 1, and so on, and that At is the cash flow in year t, at which point the project is considered to be terminated. The values of A_1, .., At are not necessarily the same, as was the case in the last chapter. The *net present value* of expenditures and revenues of the project is then:

$$A_0 + dA_1 + d^2A_2 + ... + d^tA_t,$$

where $d = \dfrac{1}{1+r}$, and r is the interest rate for discount purposes.

This is applied to the $1,000 bond with a price of $1,075, an interest rate of 5%, and a term of 10 years, with an interest rate for discount purposes of 4%. In this case the cash flow in the years 1–10 happens to be constant. Panel 8.1 gives the discounted cash flow, consisting of the discounted interest revenues and the discounted repayment of the principal. Cell C7 contains the formula =B7/(1+DIR)^A7, which is copied downwards. The sum of the discounted cash flow is $6.11, which means that this bond is a good investment if the return on a savings account for 10 years is 4%.

Instead of determining the present value of each cash flow and summing the result, the spreadsheet function NPV can be used, which has the general form:

=NPV(Interest Rate,Range).

In our example, this would be, see cell E7:

$= NPV(DIR,B7:B17) = \$5.87.$

This differs from the amount $6.11 which was found in cell C19. The reason for this is that the NPV spreadsheet function *discounts the cash flows back to one period before the first cash flow*, as in the PV function. Compared with the *usual net present value* (UNPV), the NPV discounts the cash flow one period back too far. To obtain the UNPV, the NPV should be brought one period forward, which is done by multiplying by 1+r:

UNPV = (1+DIR)*NPV(). (1)

Panel 8.1 Calculation of Present Value of $1,000 Bond

	A	B	C	D	E	F	G
1	Amount	A	$1,000	PV Interest	$406	=PV(DIR,10,-IR*A)	
2	Int. Rate	IR	5%	PV Rep. Prin.	$676	=A/(1+DIR)^10	
3	Price	PR	$1,075	Price	($1,075)	=-P	
4	Disc. IR	DIR	4%	Sum	$6.11	=SUM(F1:F3)	
5							
6		Year	Cashflow	Disc. CF			
7		0	($1,075)	($1,075)	NPV	$5.87	=NPV(DIR,B7:B17)
8		1	$50	$48	UNPV	$6.11	=(1+DIR)*NPV(DIR,B7:B17)
9		2	$50	$46	UNPV	$6.11	=B7+NPV(C4,B8:B17)
10		3	$50	$44			
11		4	$50	$43			
12		5	$50	$41			
13		6	$50	$40			
14		7	$50	$38			
15		8	$50	$37			
16		9	$50	$35			
17		10	$1,050	$709			
18							
19	Sum		$425	$6.11			

Alternatively, we may use:

$$UNPV = A_0 + NPV(r, A_1:A_n),$$

where A_0 is the first cash flow and $A_1:A_n$ the range of the remainder. This is illustrated in cells E8 and E9, which use these formulas.

The net present value of the bond cashflow can also be determined as sum of the present values of the interest payments, the principal repayments, and the bond purchase price. This calculation is performed in the range E1:E4, and results in the same value.

8.3 Application to a Real Estate Project

As another example may be taken the purchase of a condominium complex. The purchase price is $1,000,000 and renovations cost $200,000. The complex is going to be rented out for 10 years, yielding an annual net revenue of $120,000 increasing at 5% per year, after which it is sold for $1,500,000. The net present value should be determined for discount interest rates of 6%, 12%, and 20%.

Panel 8.2 gives the expenditures and revenues in the various years, as well as their present value at the start of the first year for the various interest rates. Cell B10 is entered as =B9*(1+$RIP), which is copied downwards. Cell C8 is entered as =$B8/(1+C$7)^$A8, which is copied to the range C8:E18. In row 19 summation is used to give the net present values of the entire project for different discount interest rates. The amounts in C19:E19 can also be obtained independently using the NPV function, see the formula for C20 in C21.

Panel 8.2 Net Present Value for Project

	A	B	C	D	E
1	P. Price	PP	$1,000,000		
2	Renovation	RN	$200,000		
3	S. Price	SP	$1,500,000		
4	Revenue	REV	$120,000		
5	Rev. Inc. %	RIP	5%		
6					
7	Year	Cashflow	6%	12%	20%
8	0	($1,200,000)	($1,200,000)	($1,200,000)	($1,200,000)
9	1	$120,000	$113,208	$107,143	$100,000
10	2	$126,000	$112,140	$100,446	$87,500
11	3	$132,300	$111,082	$94,169	$76,563
12	4	$138,915	$110,034	$88,283	$66,992
13	5	$145,861	$108,996	$82,765	$58,618
14	6	$153,154	$107,967	$77,592	$51,291
15	7	$160,811	$106,949	$72,743	$44,880
16	8	$168,852	$105,940	$68,197	$39,270
17	9	$177,295	$104,940	$63,934	$34,361
18	10	$1,686,159	$941,543	$542,898	$272,324
19	Sum	$1,809,347	$722,797	$98,170	($368,202)
20	UNPV		$722,797	$98,170	($368,202)
21			=(1+C7)*NPV(C7,$B$8:$B$18)		

Panel 8.3 Undiscounted and Discounted Cash Flows

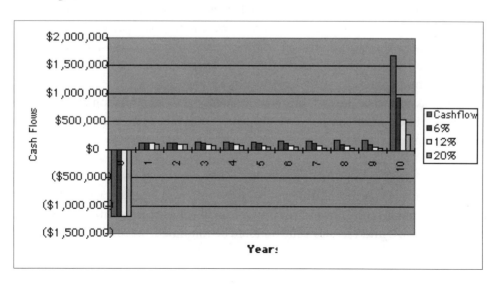

After 10 years the net cash flow is $1,809,347, but the net present value varies according to the interest rate used. At 6% the project seems interesting, at 12% it is borderline, while for 20% the project is definitely unattractive.

Panel 8.3 illustrates graphically the differences between the undiscounted cashflows and the cashflows discounted at different interest rates.

8.4 The Appropriate Interest Rate for Discount Purposes

Since the net present value changes drastically for different interest rates, the appropriate interest rate to be used for the evaluation of a project should be carefully selected. This interest rate should be equal to the opportunity cost of the use of money or capital for the various years, which means that it should be equal to the best return money can earn in the years concerned if it is financed by money to be withdrawn from other investments, or to the lowest cost of financing, if it is financed by additional borrowing. The net present value formula implies that this interest rate is constant for any amount of money required, and that it is the same in every year. These assumptions are not always satisfied.

But a rather typical situation is that the project is one among a number of other projects of the same company, and that this company has set a certain rate of interest that should be achieved. This rate may be used to determine the present value.

Such a rate of interest may consist of a number of components:

1. the real return component

2. the inflation component

3. the uncertainty component

If inflation is 5% per year, any investor will expect returns to cover at least inflation, since otherwise investment in gold or less inflation prone currencies is more attractive. Also a real return, that is a return above inflation, is expected. Furthermore, since the data for the expenditures and revenues used in the project evaluation are just estimates, and the realization may be different, investors, who are mostly risk averse, want to be compensated for the uncertainty by a higher return.

Let us assume that the real return component is 7%, the inflation component is 5%, and the uncertainty component is 4%. This means that an investment of $1 in one year should give

$$(1+0.07)(1+0.05)(1+0.04) = 1.16844,$$

so that r = 16.844%, which is different from the sum of the percentages, 16%. These percentages are therefore not additive, but for small percentages addition gives a good approximation. If interest rates a and b should be combined, the resulting interest rate is given by

$$(1+a)(1+b)-1 = a+b+ab,$$

whereas simple addition gives a + b, so that the underestimation error is ab. For a = 5% and b = 2%, ab = 0.1%, which can usually be neglected, but for a = b = 10%, ab = 1%, which is not insignificant any more.

It often occurs that decision makers do not know precisely the appropriate interest rate. In these cases the net present value for a number of interest rates may be given. For example, in the condominium case the net present values for r = 10%, 15%, and 20% may be required.

8.5 The Internal Rate of Return

For the condominium example the net present value for interest rates of 6%, 12% and 20% were $722,797, $98,170 and –$368,202. Decision makers may wish to know at what interest rate does the net present value become equal to 0. This interest rate is called the *internal rate of return* (IRR), because money invested in the project has a return of precisely that rate. If elsewhere a higher rate can be obtained for money invested, the project is obviously not attractive, but the rate is higher than that of alternative investments, the project is advantageous.

Panel 8.4 illustrates the determination of the internal rate of return in more detail. Cell D10 contains the formula =(1+C10)*NPV(C10,$B$10:$B$20), which is copied to D10:D20. From the result it can be concluded that the IRR is between 12% and 14% and is probably between 13% and 13.5%.

Panel 8.5 illustrates results for interest rates varying by 2% from 0% to 20%. At about 13.3% the curve crosses the horizontal axis, so that this must be the internal rate of return.

For the same interest rate, the acceptance or rejection of a project based on the internal rate of return is the same as that based on the net present value.

No explicit expression can be given for the internal rate of return, but it can be calculated by iteration. For a particular rate of interest, the net present value is calculated. If it is positive, it is recalculated for a higher interest rate, and so on, until the net present value approaches 0. The internal rate of return is not necessarily unique, which means that there may be projects that have a zero net present value for different interest rates. The internal rate of return is unique if the first cash flow is negative and all others positive. For almost all practical applications there is only one usable internal rate of return.

For the internal rate of return function IRR the spreadsheet uses an iteration procedure which starts with a guess for the rate. This rate, called Guess, is the second argument of the function. The first argument is the range of the cash flow:

IRR(*Range,Guess*).

This is applied in the spreadsheet of Panel 8.4, where cell D20 has the formula =IRR(B8:B18, 10%), which results in 13.31%.

Panel 8.4 Net Present Value, Discount Interest Rate, and Internal Rate of Return

	A	B	C	D
1	Data			
2	P. Price	PP	$1,000,000	
3	Renovation	RN	$200,000	
4	S. Price	SP	$1,500,000	
5	Revenue	REV	$120,000	
6	Rev. Inc. %	RIP	5%	
7				
8	Cashflows			
9	Year	Cashflow	DIR	UNPV
10	0	($1,200,000)	0%	$1,809,347
11	1	$120,000	2%	$1,375,566
12	2	$126,000	4%	$1,018,420
13	3	$132,300	6%	$722,797
14	4	$138,915	8%	$476,817
15	5	$145,861	10%	$271,092
16	6	$153,154	12%	$98,170
17	7	$160,811	14%	($47,897)
18	8	$168,852	16%	($171,877)
19	9	$177,295	18%	($277,610)
20	10	$1,686,159	20%	($368,202)
21	Sum	$1,809,347		
22			IRR	13.31%

Panel 8.5 Net Present Value and Internal Rate of Return

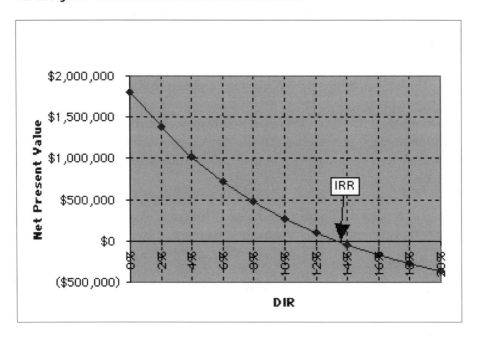

As with the NPV function, this function discounts the cash flows back to the period before the first cash flow, but this does not influence the result, since, according to equation (1) above, if NPV = 0, then UNPV = 0, so that the function is also valid if we wish to discount back to the period of the first cash flow.

The net present value and the internal rate of return are only some of the criteria used for project selection. Another is, for example, the *payback period*, which is the number of years it takes before accumulated revenues exceed accumulated expenditures. But decisions will also be influenced by many other factors, such as the opinions of decision makers regarding the data used in the project evaluation and the general economic situation. The main criteria for project evaluation, net present value and internal rate of return, can therefore be best regarded as *decision support* tools.

Exercises

8.1 Suppose a project is delayed by one or more years. If all amounts and rates are given with reference to the starting year, how will this delay affect the present value and the internal rate of return?

8.2 How would you deal with a situation in which the interest rate for present value purposes is 9% for year 1, 10% for the years 2–5, and 11% for the years 6–10? Apply this to the condominium example of this chapter.

Assignments

8.1 The Duplex Case

A person considers buying a duplex. The purchase price is $100,000, and legal and other costs are $5,000. A mortgage of $60,000 at 13% interest can be taken out, which will be amortized in 10 years with equal payments (for the sum of interest and mortgage repayment) every year.

The rental income for the first year is estimated at $6,000, and for the second year at $12,000. For all later years the rent is assumed to increase by 6% per year. The annual maintenance costs were $1,000 in the first year, and should be adjusted for inflation in later years. Painting is necessary in years 1, 6, and 10 and costs $3,500 in Year 1, to be adjusted for inflation in later years. Property taxes are in the first year $1,000 and are increasing with inflation. The property is planned to be sold after 10 years for an amount net of selling costs of $200,000. Inflation is expected to be 5% per year.

Create a spreadsheet for this project and determine its net present value and internal rate of return. The spreadsheet should consist of a data section, a results section, and a cash flow calculations section. The last section should contain for all years the rental income, the mortgage payment, the outstanding mortgage, the mortgage interest, the mortgage repayment, and the various expenditures. The results section should contain the cash flow, the present values at 10, 15, and 20%, and the internal rate of return.

8.2 The Financial Returns of a Degree

A person intends to start in the coming year a 4-year program for a BA(Econ) and wishes to determine the costs and benefits of this study, at least as far as these can be expressed monetarily. Tuition and compulsory fees will be $1,200 in the first year and are expected to rise in the following years by 7.5% per year. Books cost $500 per year in the first year and will increase by inflation which is estimated at 5% per year. To study, a job has to be given up with a net income of $12,000 per year in the first year, with annual increases equal to inflation. Annual spending for consumption is assumed to be equal to the income of this job, irrespective of whether the person keeps this job or studies and finds a better job. A study loan is available of $5,000 per year in all four years, which is interest free until the completion of the study, at which point only two-thirds has to be paid back. In addition to this, money is assumed to be available for borrowing and may be deposited at 10% interest.

Once the degree has been obtained, it is expected that a position can be obtained with a starting salary which is 30% more than the income would have been for the previous job. Moreover, the salary increases by 6% per year. It is assumed that this person will work in this position for 30 years.

(a) Find for the years of study the various costs, the total costs, the contribution made by the study loan, and the total costs after the study loan has been taken into account. Also find the present value of these costs and the percentages of the total costs for the various kinds of costs and the study loan.

(b) Find the benefits of the degree for the years that the person will have the position.

(c) After combining the costs and benefits, determine the net present value and the internal rate of return of taking the degree.

Create a well-organized spreadsheet to answer the following questions, with a data section and a summary section, and use range names. Protect the entire spreadsheet except the data. Print the spreadsheet.

8.3 Inflation and Fixed Income

To obtain a perspective on the effect of inflation on people with fixed incomes, let us look at a couple that at the beginning of 1971 had $100,000 in cash, with which they bought a 17-year annuity with monthly payments. The interest rate was 8%.

(a) What is the monthly amount of the payments?

(b) Retrieve the Consumer Price Index for Calgary for the years 1971–1987 from the CANSIM Database on the disk accompanying this book.

(c) Transfer these data to your worksheet.

(d) Which amounts at the end of 1987 are equivalent in terms of purchasing power to the $100,000 and the monthly annuity payment in 1971?

(e) Determine the annual inflation percentage for each of the years from 1971 to

1987.

(f) Graph this annual inflation rate and print the graph.

(g) Determine the purchasing power of the monthly payment in terms of January 1971 dollars over the period 1971–1980, graph it, and print the graph. What is the average purchasing power over this period?

(h) Suppose an annuity with monthly payments that are the same in terms of purchasing power can be set up, assuming that the inflation over the period 1971–1987 could have been predicted exactly. What would, for such annuity with a present value of $100,000 at the start of 1971, the monthly payment be at the start of 1971?

8.4 Jail Privatization

Assume that the Provincial Government wants to privatize jails and that it invites bids to run the Calgary jail for 5 years. The file T1DATA, on the accompanying disk, contains the average number of inmates forecasted for each month in the years 1–5. All data are fictitious.

The spreadsheet should be well-organized and the various parts should be appropriately formatted. Data sections and range names should be used to enhance the presentation.

Create a well-organized spreadsheet, with the various parts appropriately formatted, to answer the following questions.

(a) Assume that the government will pay $32 per inmate-day. Determine the total number of inmate-days for each year and for the entire 5-year period and the corresponding totals to be paid out. Assume that all months have 30.5 days. Also determine the average number of inmates and the corresponding percentage increase for each year.

(b) Assume that the forecasts have a 10% error in the sense that the actual values may be 10% higher (high values) or 10% lower (low values). The payment per inmate-day may also vary from $30–$40. Make up a table using the high values for the expected payments in each year and the total payment over the 5-year period for payment per man-day at $40, $41, :, $50. Do the same for the low values.

(c) Assume that the payments for Year1 are made in one single payment at the end of the year at $32 per inmate-day. If the discount interest rate (with no compounding) is 10% per year, what is the net present value of this payment at the start of Year 1 (the end of Year 0)? What is the comparable net present value if payments are made at the end of each month? What is the difference?

(d) To run the jail, a manager is required earning $65,000 per year and two assistant managers earning $40,000 per year each. One supervisor and four security guards are required 24 hours per day, the former earning $25 per hour and the latter $15 per hour. They work 1,750 hours per year. Daytime guards are required during 16 hours per day, and there should be one guard per 40 inmates, based on the average annual number of inmates. These guards earn $12 per hour and work 1,750 hours per year. Benefits on salaries and wages are 15%. Medical and legal services costs total $250,000. Inmate food and supplies are $18 per day per inmate. Utilities and maintenance are estimated at $280,000 per year. Hourly paid staff may work overtime at the same rates to absorb noninteger numbers of staff. Make up annual expenditure budgets for the years 1–5. How many of the hourly paid staff are required?

(e) Give a summary of expenditures and receipts for each year. Assuming that start-up costs incurred in the year before the first year are $500,000, find the net present value and the internal rate of return of running the jail for five years. Do the same if after Year 1 the receipts increase by 5% per year.

Chapter 9
Cash Flow Analysis

This chapter continues the treatment of project evaluation and deals with various cash flow profiles and cash balances for a project. First the discounted cash flow profile is considered and compared with the undiscounted cash flow. The discounted cash flow is also expressed as a percentage of the initial outlay. How much money is tied up in a project is given by cash balances. Both straight and discounted cash balances are considered. The last part of the chapter discusses project financing with various loans.

9.1 Discounted Cash Flow

To discuss various aspects of the cash flow of a project, consider the following example, which concerns a real estate project requiring an initial expenditure of $200,000 and another $100,000 after one year. In years 2–9 net revenues are $60,000, increasing at 5% per year. In Year 10 the entire project is sold at a price of $250,000. The project should be evaluated using a discount interest rate of 15%.

Panel 9.1 gives the spreadsheet for an analysis of this project. The first six rows contain the data, which have been given range names as indicated. Consequently, cell B10 contains the formula =–IC*2/3, cell B11 the formula =–IC/3, cell B12 the formula NR*(1+IP)^(A12–2), all of which are copied downwards. The discounted cash flow is obtained for C10 as =B10/(1+DIR)^A10 which is copied downwards. Its sum is $44,588 (see cell F2), which can also be obtained using the NPV function, which is determined by the formula =NPV(DIR,B10:B20)*(1+DIR). The internal rate of return is found in cell F3 which contains =IRR(B10:B20,10%). The remaining columns are explained below.

The present value of this project at 15% interest is $44,588, and the internal rate of return is 18%. This means that the project is viable and profitable, and should therefore be undertaken. However, it is advisable not just to look at these two overall measures of profitability, but to consider the entire cash flow profile.

As amounts in later years are less important than those in earlier years, instead of the cash flow, the *discounted* cash flow should be considered, see range C9:C22 in Panel 9.1. Panel 9.2 displays both cash flows graphically. From this discounted cash flow it is clear that the final selling price $250,000 is worth only $61,796, so that its contribution is less important than the initial expenditure amounts and the returns in the earlier years. Keeping initial costs down is obviously crucial. A cost overrun of 20% ($40,000) in the first year can wipe out almost the entire present value of the project.

To obtain an idea of the relative size of expenditures and revenues in the various years, the discounted cash flows may be expressed as percentages of the discounted expenditures of the first two years. The result is given in the Cashflow Percentage

Panel 9.1 Cash Flows and Cash Balances of Real Estate Project

	A	B	C	D	E	F
1	Data				Results	
2	Initial Costs	IC	$300,000		NPV	$44,588
3	Net Revenue	NR	$60,000		IRR	18%
4	Disc.Int.Rate	DIR	15%			
5	N.Rev.Incr.%	IP	5%			
6	Final Payme	FP	$250,000			
7						
8	Cashflows					
9	Year	Cashflow	Disc.CF	CF %	Cash Bal.	I.B.Cash B.
10	0	($200,000)	($200,000)	-70%	($200,000)	($200,000)
11	1	($100,000)	($86,957)	-30%	($300,000)	($330,000)
12	2	$60,000	$45,369	16%	($240,000)	($319,500)
13	3	$63,000	$41,424	14%	($177,000)	($304,425)
14	4	$66,150	$37,821	13%	($110,850)	($283,939)
15	5	$69,458	$34,533	12%	($41,393)	($257,072)
16	6	$72,930	$31,530	11%	$31,538	($222,702)
17	7	$76,577	$28,788	10%	$108,115	($179,531)
18	8	$80,406	$26,285	9%	$188,521	($126,055)
19	9	$84,426	$23,999	8%	$272,947	($60,537)
20	10	$250,000	$61,796	22%	$522,947	$180,382
21						
22	Total	$522,947	$44,588	16%		

Panel 9.2 Cashflow and Discounted Cashflow Profile

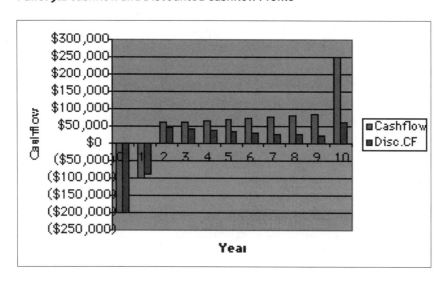

column of Panel 9.1 (D9:D22). Seventy percent of the expenditures took place at the start of the project, and 30% after one year. Sizteen percent of the expenditures is recovered in Year 2, but this percentage declines in subsequent years because the inflation adjustment of 5% is much less than the 15% interest rate used for discounting. The revenues of Year 9 are 8% of expenditures. The final sale in Year 10 provides only 22% of initial costs.

Summing up all percentages results in 16%, which is the present value expressed as a percentage of discounted costs. This can be considered as another measure of profitability.

9.2 Cash Balances

The cash flow analysis using present value and internal rate of return does not consider explicitly how the project is financed. It implicitly assumes that, at the interest rate for discount purposes or at the internal rate of return, an amount of capital is available sufficient to finance the project. This means that either the company has a large internal pool of capital available with an opportunity costs equal to the interest rate, or that it can borrow from its bank sufficient amounts of money at this interest rate. In many cases this is not or not entirely realistic. The amounts of money tied up in a project over various years are usually of considerable interest to decisionmakers.

These amounts are given by the *cash balances* which equal the accumulated cash flow at any point of time. For the project concerned, these cash balances are given in the range E9:E20 in Panel 9.1. Earlier it was indicated that such an accumulated cash flow is easily created by copying formulas in a spreadsheet. Note that the final cash balance, $522,947, should equal the total of the undiscounted cash flow. These cash balances give for each year the total amount of money invested in the project. The first point of interest is the *maximum amount invested* in the project, and *when* this occurs. For the example this is $300,000 in Year 1. This means that at least this amount of financing should be available in Year 1. The second point of interest is when the cash balance becomes positive, which is called the payback period. For the example this is Year 6, so that the *payback period* is 6 years.

However, cash balances do not take into account the interest due on negative cash balances or the interest earnings from positive ones. It is therefore more appropriate to use *Interest Based Cash Balances* which is equivalent to the balance of a bank account charging interest on negative balances and paying interest on positive ones, using the discount interest rate. Such a balance is obtained at any point of time by taking the previous balance, adding interest to it, and then adding the current cash flow. The last column (F9:F20) of Panel 9.1 gives these cash balances. Cell F10 contains the formula =B10+(1+DIR)*F9, which is copied downwards.

The final amount of this cash balance is $180,382 in Year 10, which is the future value of the project. By discounting it back to Year 0, we find

$$180382^*(1/1.15)^\wedge11 = \$\,44{,}588,$$

which is the present value of the project.

Negative cash balances may be interpreted as minus the amounts of capital invested in the project. Panel 9.3 displays the interest based cash balances for the project. These amounts give a good indication of the financing needs originating from the project and also of the risk exposure due to the project. Risk is incurred because at any point of time there is always the chance that further revenue of the project will be diminished or may be entirely cut off.

Panel 9.3 Interest Based Cash Balances

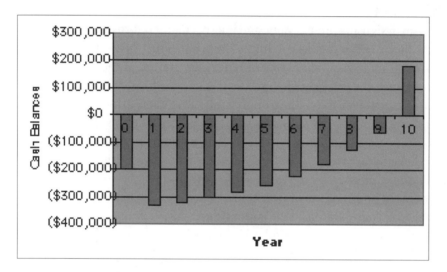

Also this cash balance has two interesting points. The first one is the amount and timing of the most negative balance, in this case $330,000 in Year 1, which indicates the maximum investment in the project. The other point is the first time this cash balance becomes positive, which happens in Year 10. This may be called the *Interest Based Payback Period*.

9.3 Project Financing

So far it was implicitly assumed that the project was financed entirely by the decision-makers, which means that only they provide the negative cash flow and receive the positive cash flow of the project. In many cases it is possible to take out loans to finance the project partly. If the interest rates of the loans are lower than the discount interest rate, this will increase the present value and the internal rate of return.

Consider the example used earlier, but assume now that the annual revenues are $44,000 instead of $60,000, which will make the present value negative at –$27,345, and decrease the internal rate of return to 13%, so that the project is not attractive any more for a discount interest rate of 15%, see the column B in Panel 9.4.

Panel 9.4a Project Evaluation with Loans, Project Part

	A	B	C	D	E	F	G	H
1	Data							
2	Initial Costs		IC	$300,000	Mortgage Int.		MI	10%
3	Net Revenue		NR	$44,000	Disc.Int.Rate		DIR	15%
4	N.Rev.Incr.%		IP	5%	Bank Cr.Line		BCL	$35,000
5	Final Payment		FP	$250,000	Bank Int.		BI	12%
6	Mortg.Princ.		MP	$150,000				
7								
8	Cashflows							
9	Year	Cashflow	Mortg.CF	Bank CF	Net CF	Disc.CF	Cash Bal.	I.B.Cash B.
10	0	($200,000)	$150,000		($50,000)	($50,000)	($50,000)	($50,000)
11	1	($100,000)	($21,000)	$35,000	($86,000)	($74,783)	($136,000)	($143,500)
12	2	$44,000	($20,400)	($4,200)	$19,400	$14,669	($116,600)	($145,625)
13	3	$46,200	($19,800)	($4,200)	$22,200	$14,597	($94,400)	($145,269)
14	4	$48,510	($19,200)	($4,200)	$25,110	$14,357	($69,290)	($141,949)
15	5	$50,935	($18,600)	($4,200)	$28,135	$13,988	($41,155)	($135,105)
16	6	$53,482	($18,000)	($4,200)	$31,282	$13,524	($9,872)	($124,090)
17	7	$56,156	($17,400)	($4,200)	$34,556	$12,991	$24,684	($108,147)
18	8	$58,964	($16,800)	($4,200)	$37,964	$12,411	$62,648	($86,404)
19	9	$61,912	($16,200)	($4,200)	$41,512	$11,800	$104,161	($57,853)
20	10	$250,000	($105,600)	($39,200)	$105,200	$26,004	$209,361	$38,670
21	Total	$370,161	($123,000)	($37,800)	$209,361	$9,559		
22	NPV	($27,345)	$32,547	$5,010	$9,559			
23	IRR	13%	10%	12%	17%			

Panel 9.4b Project Evaluation with Loans, Mortgage Part

	A	B	C	D	E
25	Mortgage				
26	Year	Mortg.Pr.	Repayment	Interest	Tot. Paym.
27	1	$150,000	$6,000	15000	$21,000
28	2	$144,000	$6,000	$14,400	$20,400
29	3	$138,000	$6,000	$13,800	$19,800
30	4	$132,000	$6,000	$13,200	$19,200
31	5	$126,000	$6,000	$12,600	$18,600
32	6	$120,000	$6,000	$12,000	$18,000
33	7	$114,000	$6,000	$11,400	$17,400
34	8	$108,000	$6,000	$10,800	$16,800
35	9	$102,000	$6,000	$10,200	$16,200
36	10	$96,000	$6,000	$9,600	$15,600
37		$90,000			

Assume now that a mortgage loan of $150,000 can be taken out at the start of the project, with an interest rate of 10%. The repayments are $6,000 per year, and the outstanding principal is paid back when the project is sold after 10 years. Furthermore, it is possible to take out a bank loan of $35,000 after one year, with an interest rate of 12%. The principal of that loan is paid back when the project is sold after 10 years.

The bottom part of Panel 9.4 contains the calculations for the mortgage payments as well as the outstanding principal after 10 years. These are used to determine the mortgage cash flow in C10:C20, which starts with a positive cash flow for the proceeds of the loan of $150,000 and ends with the last payment of $15,600 plus the outstanding principal after 10 years of $90,000. The cash flow for the bank loan is found in a similar way, and is given in the range D11:D20. The net cash flow in range E10:E20 is then the sum of the cash flows of the project plus those of the loans.

The formulas for NPV and IRR in cells B22 and B23 can be copied right to cells E22 and E23. The net present value of the net cash flow is positive at $9,559, while the corresponding rate of return is 17%, which means that the project is now an acceptable one. The loans have made an unacceptable project into an attractive one. Since the net present values are the same weighted sums of the cash flows, the net present value of the net cash flow is the sum of the net present values of the first three cash flows. The cash flows of the two loans are positive, as their interest rates are lower than the discount interest rate. Especially the mortgage loan with an NPV of $32,547 gives a large boost to the NPV of the net cash flow.

Loans also reduce the large negative cash flows required for the project. The largest cash balance is $136,000, versus $300,000 without loans. This is important if the amount of money available for investment is limited.

The disadvantage of loans is that if the project outcomes are lower than expected, these losses are borne entirely by the project owners, and while the absolute amounts concerned with these losses will not be affected by loans, their relative amounts are. Borrowing makes projects more profitable, but also more risky in this sense.

Columns G and H of Panel 9.4 give the Cash Balances and the Interest Based Cash Balances, which have the same interpretation as before, namely as the accumulated amounts of money invested in the project, without or with accumulated interest. The interpretation as the amount lost if the project fails and no more revenues would be forthcoming is not valid if there are loans, as the owners would still be responsible for debts.

Assignments

9.1 Motel Investment Case

A businessman has the opportunity to buy a motel at $800,000 in December Year 1 He considers running the motel for 5 years, starting in January Year 2, and then selling it at an estimated $1,000,000. A spreadsheet should be employed to find out whether this investment is worthwhile.

The data are as follows:

- Financing. A mortgage can be obtained for $500,000 (legal costs, etc. $3,000) at an interest rate of 12%, to be paid quarterly, with a quarterly repayment of $5,000 and the remainder of the mortgage to be paid off at the sale. A bank loan for $120,000 will be taken out (loan costs $1,000) at 15% interest paid monthly, with a repayment of $2,000 per month.
- Revenues. Room rates are $50 per room and $60 for a room with kitchenette. There are 20 rooms without and 10 with a kitchenette. Room occupancy rates for both kinds of room for the months January to December (in percentages) are: 48, 35, 37, 42, 54, 65, 95, 85, 70, 45, 40, 60.
- Utility payments over the months January to December were: $3,200, $3,300, $2,600, $2,300, $2,200, $1,800, $1,900, $1,800, $2,100, $2,400, $2,800, $3,100.
- Supplies for an occupied room $3 per night, and $4 for rooms with kitchenette. In addition to this, $50 per month for the entire motel.
- Replacements and repairs are per month $20 per room without and $25 per room with kitchenette.
- Salaries are management $6,000 per month; cleaning $1,000 per month in months with occupancy rates less than 50%, otherwise $2,000 per month.
- Taxes. Local business tax is $15,000 per year, to be paid on September 1. Federal sales tax is 8% of revenues.
- Miscellaneous. Advertising costs $580 per year. Chamber of Commerce membership $120 per year. Other smaller items $350 per year. Payments are spread through the year.
- Inflation. All prices are given for Year 1. Inflation is assumed at 5% per year, which means that all prices, revenues, and taxes (if not stated as a percentage) in Year 2 are 5% higher, and so on.

Create a well-organized spreadsheet for the exploitation of the motel during the five years, which shows the monthly and yearly cash flows and the present values (at 18% interest) and internal rate of return of the entire venture. Include a graph of the discounted cash flow and the capital invested over the five years.

9.2 An Office Tower Development

A developer considers a project involving building a 300,000 ft^2 office tower. The project will take six years. The building is intended to be leased at $90 per ft^2. In the first year the business plan must be made up, with costs of $250,000. In Year 2, the site must be acquired costing $4,000,000 and the architectural design must be made, with costs of $500,000. In Year 3, construction takes place at a cost of $150,000,000. In Year 4, the building is finished and leasing starts, but on average only 40% of the space is leased in that year. In Year 5, this percentage is 75%. In Year 6, with 95% of the space leased, the building is sold at 8 times the leasing revenues for that year. The interest rate for discount purposes is 12%. All cash flows are assumed to take place at the start of the year.

(a) Using a properly formatted spreadsheet with a data section, determine the cash flow in the six years, the net present value, and the internal rate of return.

(b) Assume now that a mortgage loan is made for 90% of the cost of the site, with an interest rate of 8.5%, annual interest payments, and repayment only when the building is sold. Furthermore, to finance construction, a bank loan is taken out for 2/3 of the construction costs for one year at an interest rate of 10.5%. In Year 4 another mortgage loan is taken out with repayment when the building is sold. Include this in the cash flow and determine the resulting net present value and internal rate of return.

(c) Determine the amounts the developer himself or herself has to finance over the six years.

(d) Using a data table, find the net present value for Year 6 lease percentages varying from 60% to 100% (by 10%), and lease prices varying from $70–$120 (by $10).

Chapter 10
Sensitivity Analysis and Data Tables

This chapter explains how the sensitivity of the present value and internal rate of return with respect to various factors is determined. Also explained are the relations between sensitivity analysis and the economic concepts of derivative or slope and elasticity. The consequences of using loans are explored for variations in annual revenues.

In this chapter you will learn the following spreadsheet commands and functions:

- Data Table

10.1 Sensitivity Analysis

The main criteria for project evaluation are present value and internal rate of return. These depend directly on the cash flow, which is determined by a number of factors. In the case of the real estate project example, these are the initial expenditures ($300,000 in years 0 and 1), the earnings per year which start in Year 2 with $60,000 per year, the increase in these earnings by 5% per year, and the final payment in Year 10, $250,000. Each of these factors have been estimated, and may turn out to be different from the estimated values. It is therefore interesting to find out how sensitive present value and internal rate of return are to changes in these factors. In this case we shall look at the consequences of changes of –20%, –10%, 10%, and 20% of each of these factors separately.

The results can be arranged as in Panel 10.1. Since costs cause changes opposite to those of the other factors, we consider increases in costs together with decreases of the other factors. Results are obtained by first multiplying the initial costs in cell C2 by 1.2. The net present value and the internal rate of return in cells F2 and F3 then change to new values: –$12,804 and 14%, which *values* are copied to C27 and C32 by the command **Edit, Paste Special, Values**. Initial costs are set back to the previous value, but now the Annual Revenues cell C3 is multiplied by 0.8. The NPV and IRR are copied to C28 and C33, and so on.

It turns out that if the initial costs are 20% lower, the present value increases to more than $100,000 and the internal rate of return to 23%. On the other hand, an increase in these costs by 20% leads to a negative present value and an internal rate of return of 14%.

A decrease in annual revenues of 20% results in a negative present value and a 14% rate of return, but an increase of the same size gives a present value of around $100,000 and an internal rate of return of 22%.

It was assumed that annual revenues would increase by 5% per year. If this percentage is decreased by 20%, hence if 4% is taken, the present value is $36,948, and an increase by 20%, hence an annual increase of 6%, increases the present value to $52,502. The internal rate of return barely changes. If the final payment of $250,000 is varied in the same way, the present value varies from $32,000 to $57,000, and the internal rate of return from 17% to 19%.

Panel 10.2 gives the sensitivity of present value with respect to the four factors. It is obvious that the sensitivity with respect to initial costs and annual revenues is much larger than the sensitivity for the increase percentage and the final payment. Panel 10.3 indicates that the same is true for the sensitivity of the internal rate of return.

Panel 10.1a Sensitivity Analysis of Present Value and Internal Rate of Return

	A	B	C	D	E	F
1	Data				Results	
2	Initial Costs	IC	$300,000		NPV	$44,588
3	Net Revenue	NR	$60,000		IRR	18%
4	Disc.Int.Rate	DIR	15%			
5	N.Rev.Incr.%	IP	5%			
6	Final Payme	FP	$250,000			
7						
8	Cashflows					
9		Year	Cashflow	Disc.CF	CF %	Cash Bal.	I.B.Cash B.
10		0	($200,000)	($200,000)	-70%	($200,000)	($200,000)
11		1	($100,000)	($86,957)	-30%	($300,000)	($330,000)
12		2	$60,000	$45,369	16%	($240,000)	($319,500)
13		3	$63,000	$41,424	14%	($177,000)	($304,425)
14		4	$66,150	$37,821	13%	($110,850)	($283,939)
15		5	$69,458	$34,533	12%	($41,393)	($257,072)
16		6	$72,930	$31,530	11%	$31,538	($222,702)
17		7	$76,577	$28,788	10%	$108,115	($179,531)
18		8	$80,406	$26,285	9%	$188,521	($126,055)
19		9	$84,426	$23,999	8%	$272,947	($60,537)
20		10	$250,000	$61,796	22%	$522,947	$180,382
21							
22	Total		$522,947	$44,588	16%		

Panel 10.1b Sensitivity Analysis of Present Value and Internal Rate of Return

	A	B	C	D	E	F	G	H	I
24	Sensitivity Analysis								
25			-20%	-10%	0%	10%	20%	Slope	El.
26	Present Value								
27	Initial Costs (-)		($12,804)	$15,892	$44,588	$73,283	$101,979	0.96	6.44
28	Annual Revenues		($9,362)	$17,613	$44,588	$71,563	$98,537	4.50	6.05
29	Increase Percentage		$36,948	$40,734	$44,588	$48,510	$52,502	N/A	N/A
30	Final Payment		$32,229	$38,408	$44,588	$50,767	$56,947	0.25	1.39
31	Internal Rate of Return								
32	Initial Costs (-)		14%	16%	18%	20%	23%	N/A	N/A
33	Annual Revenues		14%	16%	18%	20%	22%	N/A	N/A
34	Increase Percentage		18%	18%	18%	18%	19%	N/A	N/A
35	Final Payment		17%	18%	18%	18%	19%	N/A	N/A

Panel 10.2 Sensitivity of Present Value for Four Factors

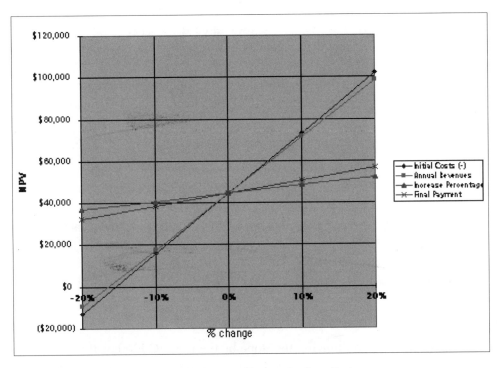

Panel 10.3 Sensitivity of the Internal Rate of Return for Four Factors

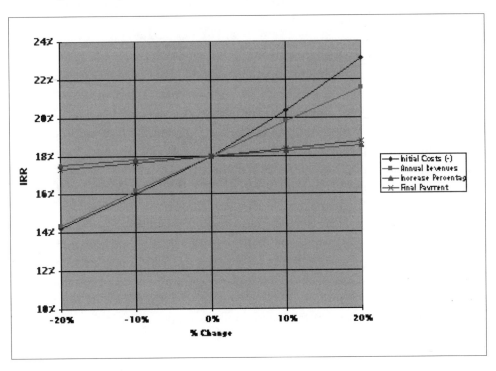

From this it may be concluded that the project, in terms of its present value and internal rate of return, is very sensitive to variations in its initial costs and annual revenues, but much less so to variations in the annual increase percentage and the final payment. Hence the first two factors should be more carefully estimated than the latter two.

Sensitivity analysis is related to the concepts of slope or derivative, and elasticity. The slope or derivative of present value with respect to initial cost is defined as

$$\frac{dPV}{dIC}$$

and can be found by calculating the change in present value due to a change in initial cost by $1. It is found to be not 1 but 0.96, because the initial costs are spread over the first two periods. An increase in annual revenue of $1 results in an increase of the present value by $4.50, whereas an increase by $1 in the final payment increases the present value by $0.25. In economics, the concept of elasticity is used, which measures the ratio of the percentage changes. For the elasticity of the present value with respect to initial costs we find:

$$\frac{dPV}{dIC} \frac{IC}{PV},$$

which is obtained by multiplying the slope by the ratio IC/PV. For the initial cost elasticity we find 6.44, for the annual revenue elasticity 6.05, and for the final payment elasticity 1.39, see Panel 10.1. For percentages the concepts of slope and elasticity have no obvious interpretation.

10.2 The Data, Table Command

The implementation of sensitivity analysis in the last section requires a fair amount of effort in changing the data concerned by the percentages and then copying the resulting values. The **Data, Table** command automates this kind of work. The Data, Table command is very powerful, and can be used in many applications. It plays the role that iterated loop statements such as FOR I = 1 TO 20 etc., have in computer languages such as BASIC and FORTRAN and are used extensively in the following chapters. There are three variants, of which the first one has a column input cell, the second a row input cell, and the third has both a column and a row input cell. First the variant with the column input cell is discussed.

Data, Table with a column input cell displays the values of one or more formulas for one column of arguments. Suppose we wish to display the future values of $1,000 deposited at an interest rate of 8% for terms varying from 5–30 years, both for annual compounding and for continuous compounding. The setup for this command is explained using Panel 10.4. The formula for annual compounding is

$=1000*1.08\wedge t,$

and that for continuous compounding

=1000*EXP(0.08*t).

These formulas are entered into C3 and D3, with for the value of t the cell B2, which is called the *input cell*. The values over which t is to vary, the arguments, are entered in the range B4:B9. The range B3:D9 is the *Table Range* (bordered), of which the range C4:D9 is to contain the desired values. Cell B3 plays no role in Data Table with a column input cell.

Panel 10.4 Setup of Data, Table with a Column Input

	A	B	C	D	E	F
1						
2	Input Cell	5				
3			$1,469	$1,492	Cells Evaluated	
4		5				
5	Arguments	10				
6		15				
7		20			Table Range	
8		25				
9		30				

First the formulas for the two cells to be evaluated and the arguments must be entered in the ranges C3:D3 and B4:B9, then the Table Range B3:D9 is selected and the Data, Table command is invoked, after which column input cell is entered. The spreadsheet then constructs an array formula in C4:D9 which it calls {=TABLE(,B2)} in which the arguments B4:B9 are put into the cells C3:D3. This is an array function, which means that no part of it can be deleted or otherwise manipulated, but only the entire array C4:D9 can be deleted or otherwise changed. The resulting numerical display can be found in Panel 10.5. Note the formula in each of the cells of C4:D9.

Panel 10.5 Result of Data, Table with a Column Input

	A	B	C	D	E	F
1						
2	Input Cell	5				
3			$1,469	$1,492	Cells Evaluated	
4		5	$ 1,469	$ 1,492		
5	Arguments	10	$ 2,159	$ 2,226	{=TABLE(,B2)}	
6		15	$ 3,172	$ 3,320		
7		20	$ 4,661	$ 4,953	Table Range	
8		25	$ 6,848	$ 7,389		
9		30	$ 10,063	$ 11,023		

Except for the impact on the display of the evaluated cells C3 and D3, the content of the input cell plays no role, but in order to check the formulas in C3 and D3 it may be given the value of the first argument. The location is not important either, except that it should not be within the table range. If there are no reasons to use a cell elsewhere, it is convenient to put it just above the table. The number of cells to be evaluated can be as large as required. The array formulas resulting from the Data, Table command require relatively large amounts of memory, so that large data tables should be avoided.

Data Tables with a row input are similar to those with a column input, except that the role of arguments and cells evaluated is interchanged.

In Data, Table command with both a column and a row input one formula is evaluated for two arguments. Consider the future value of $1,000 for varying terms and varying interest rates, which has as formula

=1000*(1+r)^t.

Panel 10.6 gives the setup for Data Table with a column and a row input. The evaluated cell is B4 with the formula

Panel 10.6. Setup for Data Table with a Column and a Row Input

	A	B	C	D	E	F	G
1							
2	Input Cells	8%	5				
3					Arguments		
4	Evaluated Cell	$ 1,469	8%	9%	10%	11%	
5		5					
6		10					
7	Arguments	15					Table Range
8		20					
9		25					
10		30					

Panel 10.7 Results of Data Table with Column and Row Inputs

	A	B	C	D	E	F	G
1							
2	Input Cells	8%	5				
3					Arguments		
4	Evaluated Cell	$ 1,469	8%	9%	10%	11%	
5		5	$ 1,469	$ 1,539	$ 1,611	$ 1,685	{=TABLE(B2,C2)}
6		10	$ 2,159	$ 2,367	$ 2,594	$ 2,839	
7	Arguments	15	$ 3,172	$ 3,642	$ 4,177	$ 4,785	Table Range
8		20	$ 4,661	$ 5,604	$ 6,727	$ 8,062	
9		25	$ 6,848	$ 8,623	$ 10,835	$ 13,585	
10		30	$ 10,063	$ 13,268	$ 17,449	$ 22,892	

$=1000*(1+C2)\wedge B2$

which is situated in the North-West corner of the table range B4:F10. In addition to the arguments for t in B5:B10, there are now the arguments for r in C4:F4.

Data Table with a column and a row input is started by selecting the table range B4:F10, after which the command Data, Table is invoked, and the row and column input cells B2 and C2 are entered. This results in the array function {=TABLE(B2,C2)} in the range C5:F10, see Panel 10.7.

For the two examples, the Data, Table commands seem of limited value, because the same results could have been obtained by copying. For example, if in Panel 10.6, the formula

$=1000*(1+C\$4)\wedge \$B5$

is entered in C5, and copied to C5:F10, the same results are obtained. However, these examples were used just for an initial explanation of the command. In the following examples copying could not have been used, as the arguments do not have a direct impact on the evaluated cells, but indirect ones via the remainder of the spreadsheet.

10.3 Sensitivity Analysis Using the Data, Table Command

Consider again the example used for sensitivity analysis in section 10.1. The relevant data are displayed in rearranged form in Panel 10.8. Cell E9 contains the formula for net present value based on the cash flow in B2:B12, and F9 the internal rate of return based on the same cash flow.

Consider sensitivity analysis with respect to initial costs. The values corresponding with changes of initial costs of –20%, –10%, :, +20% are $240,000, $270,000, ..., $360,000, are the arguments of Data Table with a column input, which are entered in the range D10:D14. The table range for Data Table is now D9:F14, and the evaluated cells are E9 and F9, which contain the formulas for NPV,

$=NPV(DIR,B2:B12)*(1+DIR)$

and for IRR,

$=IRR(B2:B12,0.1).$

As input cell is chosen the data cell for initial cost, F2. Note that the cells to be evaluated, E9 and F9, are not direct functions of the input cell, but indirect ones, via the cash flows B2:B12.

When the command Data, Table with column input is invoked, the spreadsheet will take the first argument, $240,000, and put it into the input cell E2. Then it will recalculate the entire spreadsheet, recalculating the cash flows B4:B12, and then the new values of the net present value and the internal rate of return in the evaluated cells

PART 3 Project Evaluation

E9 and F9 and store these temporarily. The same is done for the next argument, $270,000 and so on, until the last value of the argument has been dealt with. Then the calculated values are displayed in E10:F14, see Panel 10.9.

The range E10:F14 contains the array formula {=TABLE(,F2)}. Any change in the cash flow or data will immediately be reflected in the values of the array E10:F14. This is an improvement on what was done in section 10.1, where the results of the sensitivity analysis consisted of unchanging values.

Panel 10.8 Data Table Setup for Sensitivity Analysis

	A	B	C	D	E	F
1	Year	Cashflow		Data		
2	0	($200,000)		Initial Costs	IC	$ 300,000
3	1	($100,000)		Net Revenue	NR	$60,000
4	2	$60,000		Disc.Int.Rate	DIR	15%
5	3	$63,000		N.Rev.Incr.%	IP	5%
6	4	$66,150		Final Payment	FP	$250,000
7	5	$69,458				
8	6	$72,930			NPV	IRR
9	7	$76,577			$44,588	18%
10	8	$80,406		$240,000		
11	9	$84,426		$270,000		
12	10	$250,000		$300,000		
13				$330,000		
14				$360,000		

Panel 10.9 Result of Data Table with Column Input

	A	B	C	D	E	F
1	Year	Cashflow		Data		
2	0	($200,000)		Initial Costs	IC	$ 300,000
3	1	($100,000)		Net Revenue	NR	$60,000
4	2	$60,000		Disc.Int.Rate	DIR	15%
5	3	$63,000		N.Rev.Incr.%	IP	5%
6	4	$66,150		Final Payment	FP	$250,000
7	5	$69,458				
8	6	$72,930			NPV	IRR
9	7	$76,577			$44,588	18%
10	8	$80,406		$240,000	$ 101,979	23%
11	9	$84,426		$270,000	$ 73,283	20%
12	10	$250,000		$300,000	$ 44,588	18%
13				$330,000	$ 15,892	16%
14				$360,000	$ (12,804)	14%
15					{=TABLE(,F2)}	

Panel 10.10 Set-Up for Initial Cost Variation in Percentages

	A	B	C	D	E	F
1	Year	Cashflow		Data		
2	0	($160,000)		Initial Costs	IC	$ 240,000
3	1	($80,000)		Net Revenue	NR	$ 60,000
4	2	$60,000		Disc.Int.Rate	DIR	15%
5	3	$63,000		N.Rev.Incr.%	IP	5%
6	4	$66,150		Final Payment	FP	$ 250,000
7	5	$09,458				
8	6	$72,930		-20%	NPV	IRR
9	7	$76,577			$101,979	23%
10	8	$80,406		-20%		
11	9	$84,426		-10%		
12	10	$250,000		0%		
13				10%		
14				20%		

It is also possible to use the change percentages −20%, −10%, ... directly as arguments in the Data Table. This is illustrated in Panel 10.10. The change percentages are entered as arguments in D10:D14. Cell F2, which represents initial costs, is given the formula

=300000*(1+D8)

where D8 is the input cell for the percentages. The results of Data Table with D8 as column input cell are the same as before.

Of the 40 items of sensitivity analysis of Panel 10.1, groups of 10 can be generated at the same time. The arrangement in columns can be transposed, or changed into an arrangement in rows used in Panel 10.1 by the **Copy** command and then the command **Edit, Paste Special, Transpose**.

The Data, Table command can be used for sensitivity analysis of two factors simultaneously. For example, the sensitivity of the internal rate of return with respect to variations of initial costs and net revenue may be determined. The setup for the Data, Table command is given in Panel 10.11. The evaluated cell E9 contains =IRR(B2:B12,0.1). First the actual values of initial costs and net revenue are varied. The data cells for Initial Costs in F2 and for Net Revenue in F3 are used as input cells for the arguments of initial costs in E10:E14 and those for net revenue in F9:J9. The table range is E9:J14.

Inspecting the results of the Data, Table command, we find in F10:J14 a minimum rate of return of 11% when costs are 20% higher and revenues 20% lower, whereas a maximum of 27% is obtained in the opposite case.

It is also possible to use percentage arguments, see Panel 10.12. In this case initial costs in E2 are given the formula =300000*(1+E8) and net revenue in E3, =60000*(1+F8), where E8 and F8 are the input cells for the percentage arguments. The results are the same as in Panel 10.11.

Panel 10.11 Two-Factor Sensitivity Analysis

	A	B	C	D	E	F	G	H	I	J
1	Year	Cashflow		Data						
2	0	($200,000)		Initial Costs	IC	$300,000				
3	1	($100,000)		Net Revenue	NR	$ 60,000				
4	2	$80,000		Disc.Int.Rate	DIR	15%				
5	3	$63,000		N.Rev.Incr.%	IP	5%				
6	4	$66,150		Final Payment	FP	$250,000				
7	5	$69,458								
8	6	$72,930						Net Revenue		
9	7	$70,577			16%	$48,000	$54,000	$60,000	$66,000	$72,000
10	8	$80,406			$240,000	18%	21%	23%	25%	27%
11	9	$84,426		Init. Costs	$270,000	18%	18%	20%	22%	24%
12	10	$250,000			$300,000	14%	16%	18%	20%	22%
13					$320,000	13%	14%	16%	18%	19%
14					$360,000	11%	13%	14%	16%	17%
15					{=TABLE(F3,F2)}					

Panel 10.12 Two-Factor Sensitivity Analysis with Percentage Arguments

	A	B	C	D	E	F	G	H	I	J
1	Year	Cashflow		Data						
2	0	($150,000)		Initial Costs	IC	$240,000				
3	1	($80,000)		Net Revenue	NR	$ 48,000				
4	2	$48,000		Disc.Int.Rate	DIR	15%				
5	3	$50,400		N.Rev.Incr.%	IP	5%				
6	4	$52,920		Final Payment	FP	$250,000				
7	5	$55,566								
8	6	$58,344			-20%	-20%		Net Revenue		
9	7	$61,262			19%	-20%	-10%	0%	10%	20%
10	8	$64,325			-20%	19%	21%	23%	25%	27%
11	9	$67,541		Init. Costs	-10%	16%	18%	20%	22%	24%
12	10	$250,000			0%	14%	16%	18%	20%	22%
13					10%	13%	14%	16%	18%	19%
14					20%	11%	13%	14%	16%	17%
15					{=TABLE(E8,F8)}					

10.4 Loans and Sensitivity Analysis

Earlier it was shown that taking out the mortgage and bank loans was advantageous under the assumptions made, but it was also indicated that loans may lead to greater variability of measures of profitability. The Data, Table command can be used to facilitate computations for particular examples.

Consider again the real estate project, and in particular the variation in net revenue. As in most cases the final sales amount in Year 10 will be related to net revenue, assume that it varies with the net revenue in Year 2, and that it is always the same multiple 250,000/60,000 = 5.68 of this revenue. The central value of net revenue in Year 2 is $44,000, and we shall consider variations of this from −30% to 30%, varying

Panel 10.12a The Effect of Loans

	A	B	C	D	E
18	Cashflows				
19	Year	Cashflow	Mortg.CF	Bank CF	Net CF
20	0	($200,000)	$150,000		($50,000)
21	1	($100,000)	($21,000)	$35,000	($86,000)
22	2	$44,000	($20,400)	($4,200)	$19,400
23	3	$46,200	($19,800)	($4,200)	$22,200
24	4	$48,510	($19,200)	($4,200)	$25,110
25	5	$50,936	($18,600)	($4,200)	$28,136
26	6	$53,482	($18,000)	($4,200)	$31,282
27	7	$56,156	($17,400)	($4,200)	$34,556
28	8	$58,964	($16,800)	($4,200)	$37,964
29	9	$61,912	($16,200)	($4,200)	$41,512
30	10	$250,000	($105,600)	($39,200)	$105,200
31	Total	$370,161	($123,000)	($37,800)	$209,361
32	Mortgage				
33	Year	Mortg.Pr.	Repayment	Interest	T. Pmt.
34	1	$150,000	$6,000	$15,000	$21,000
35	2	$144,000	$6,000	$14,400	$20,400
36	3	$138,000	$6,000	$13,800	$19,800
37	4	$132,000	$6,000	$13,200	$19,200
38	5	$126,000	$6,000	$12,600	$18,600
39	6	$120,000	$6,000	$12,000	$18,000
40	7	$114,000	$6,000	$11,400	$17,400
41	8	$108,000	$6,000	$10,800	$16,800
42	9	$102,000	$6,000	$10,200	$16,200
43	10	$96,000	$6,000	$9,600	$15,600
44		$90,000			

Panel 10.12b The Effect of Loans

	A	B	C	D	E	F	G	H	I	J
1	Data						Data Table			
2	Initial Costs		IC	$300,000		0%	NPV-NML	NPV-ML	IRR-NML	IRR-ML
3	Net Revenue		NR	$44,000			($27,345)	$9,599	13%	17%
4	N.Rev.Incr.%		IP	5%		-30%	($105,220)	($68,325)	7%	1%
5	Final Payment		FP	$250,000		-25%	($92,248)	($55,344)	8%	4%
6	Mortg.Prino.		MP	$150,000		-20%	($79,267)	($42,364)	8%	7%
7	Mortgage Int.		MI	10%		-15%	($66,287)	($29,383)	10%	10%
8	Disc.Int.Rate		DIR	15%		-10%	($53,306)	($16,403)	11%	12%
9	Bank Cr.Line		BCL	$35,000		-5%	($40,326)	($3,422)	12%	14%
10	Bank Int		BI	12%		0%	($27,345)	$9,599	13%	17%
11	Results	Cashflow	Mortg.CF	Bank CF	Net CF	5%	($14,364)	$22,639	14%	19%
12	NPV	($27,345)	$32,647	$5,010	$9,550	10%	($1,384)	$35,620	16%	20%
13	IRR	13%	10%	12%	17%	15%	$11,597	$48,500	16%	22%
14						20%	$24,577	$61,481	17%	24%
15						25%	$37,558	$74,461	17%	26%
16						30%	$50,538	$87,442	19%	27%
17						{=TABLE(,F2)}				

by 5%, see Panel 10.12. A table range F3:J16 is used which has as cells to be evaluated, G3:J3, the net present value without and with loans, and the internal rate of return without and with loans, which are made equal to B12, E12, B13, and E13. Cell D3 contains =44000*(1–F2), where F2 is the input cell.

After the command is run, the results G4:J16 are displayed. These are best understood by using graphs. Panel 10.13 compares the net present value without and with loans, and shows that the value with loans is always a constant amount higher than that without loans. This constant amount is in fact the net present value of the mortgage and bank loans. From the perspective of the net present value with a given discount interest rate, the consequences of taking loans are always beneficial, if at least the present value of these loans is positive, which is true if the discount interest rate exceeds the loan interest rate.

Panel 10.14 displays the results for the internal rate of return. There we see for low revenues, the rate of return is lower with loans than that without loans, whereas in high revenues, the reverse is true.

This means that if the discount interest rate for enterprise is stable and does not depend on this particular project, then taking out loans is always advantageous, but if the project is a rather unique one, the lower rates of return associated with low revenues for the loans case should be weighted with higher rates of return for high revenues.

Panel 10.13 Net Present Value Without and With Loans

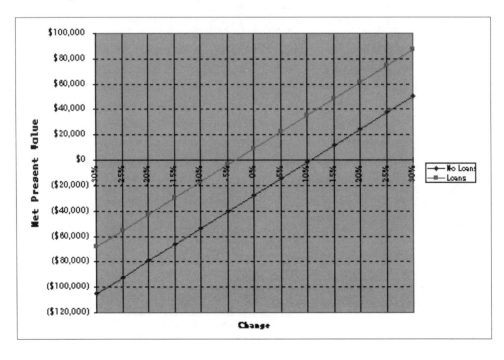

Panel 10.14 Internal Rate of Return Without and With Loans

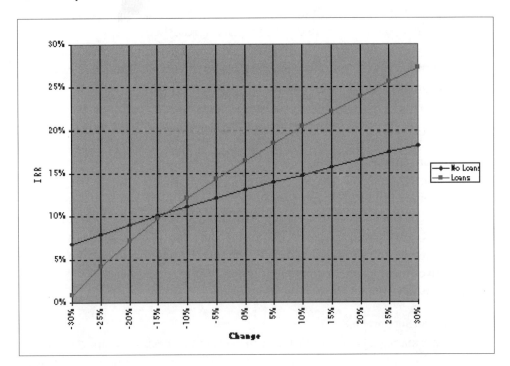

Exercises

10.1. Use the Data, Table command to generate the values underlying Panel 8.5 of Chapter 8.

Assignments

10.1 A Car Leasing Problem

A car dealer sells and leases cars. The monthly payments of car leases are based on given selling prices using the net present value of the payments and related revenues and costs.

The leasing arrangements are as follows. The lease term is three years. Monthly lease payments are made at the end of each month. At the start of the lease, a leasing deposit of 5% of the selling price is charged, which is returned at the end of the lease when the customer returns the car. At that time the customer must pay an inspection fee of $200, which approximately reflects the cost of this inspection. The residual value of a 3-year-old car is 40% of the original selling price. The interest rate for discounting purposes is 12.5%.

(a) Calculate the monthly payment for the above lease for a car with a selling price of $10,000, listing the various parts of the calculations. Use range names where appropriate. Print the relevant parts of the spreadsheet.

(b)   Determine the monthly payments in the case in which the monthly payments are not constant but adjusted for inflation, which is assumed to be 5% per year. Print the relevant part of the spreadsheet.

(c)   For constant monthly payments, make up a table using the Data, Table command which displays the monthly payments for interest rates varying from 10–15 %, by 1%, and for car prices varying from $10,000 – $30,000 varying by $2,500. Print this table.

(d)   The dealer has in the following months leased cars with the indicated selling prices:

Year 1: August $16,000

Year 2: March $22,000

Year 3: April $17,600; July $28,000

In Year 4 the leases are assumed to be the same as in Year 3, except that the prices will be 6% higher. Determine over the years 1–6 for the leasing activities the projected cash flow, the interest-based cash balance, and the investment. Print the corresponding part of the spreadsheet.

(e)   Create a suitable graph of the investment.

10.2   Decision Support Case

You are managing a small consulting firm providing decision support services to business, and your task is to make up an offer to provide these services for a period of 4 years (Year 1, 2, 3, and 4) to an oil company. It will involve placing three persons for these years in that company. One of these persons is earning $55,000 and the other two $40,000 per year in Year 1. These salaries are expected to increase by 5% at the start of each new year. After the four years are over, these persons will need 6 months for retraining and relocation, the costs of which should be included. On top of the salaries, 20% benefits have to be paid. All salaries and benefits are paid at the end of each month.

Each person must be supplied with a microcomputer which costs at the beginning of Year 1 $15,000. The value of the equipment, after it has been used for 4 years is estimated at 10% of its original value. For each microcomputer a service contract will have to be bought, which is $1,500 per year, to be paid at the start of each year.

Overhead costs (which includes part of your income) are 17.5% of personnel and computer costs.

The decision support contract with the oil company is one in which the oil company pays at the end of each month during the four years a fixed payment. The present value of these payments should be equal to the present value of total costs.

The annual interest (with annual compounding) is 15%. Months should be represented as $\frac{1}{12}$ of a year.

Build a well-organized and well-formatted spreadsheet with the various costs, the payments, the cash flow, and accumulated cash flow for each month over the four years. Also determine for each kind of cost the net present value and its percentage of the net present value of total costs.

10.3 The Economics of Schools

A plan is made to start a school with a one-year training course. The plan involves running this school for 10 years. In the first four years 20, 30, 40 and 50 students are expected to enroll, while for the remaining years the number is assumed to grow by 5% per year. Tuition is set at $6,000 per year in Year 1, which in subsequent years will grow by the expected general inflation, assumed to be 4% per year. Space is to be leased for 10 years at $80,000 per year, with no inflation adjustment. The personnel consists of the director, who will earn $60,000 per year, an administrator with a salary of $30,000, and instructors with a salary of $45,000. All salaries will go up with inflation. Each instructor can have at most 30 students. Each of the persons employed and each student must have a computer workstation, which costs $3,000 to purchase in any year (no inflation adjustment needed), and which can be used in all subsequent years. Computer maintenance and depreciation is $500 per year, increasing with inflation. The interest rate for discount purposes is 10%. No residual value is assumed to remain after 10 years.

(a) Create a well-organized and well-formatted spreadsheet to evaluate this project. Use a data section with range names. Protect the entire spreadsheet except the data cells. Calculate the present value as evaluated in the first year, and the internal rate of return. Integer amounts, where appropriate, may be obtained by using the INT() function, which returns the integer part of its argument.

(b) Calculate the interest-based cash balances for the 10 years, and graph these in a bar graph using title lines for the graph and for the X-axis and the Y-axis. Name this graph and save it for printing.

(c) Consider equal percentage changes to all enrollment numbers. Perform sensitivity analysis of the present value and the internal rate of return with respect to enrollment, with percentage changes of –20%, –10%, 0, 10%, and 20%.

(d) Use the Data, Table command to calculate the present value for tuition varying from $0–10,000 by $1,000 and the number of students per instructor varying from 10 to 50 by 5.

10.4 Aircraft Leasing

You are in the business of leasing aircraft to airlines. You are considering buying an airplane for $25,000,000. Such an airplane can be leased out to airlines for 20 years, at $3,500,000 per year, after which it can be sold for 20% of its original value. After each 3 years, the airplane must be given a major overhaul, which costs $57,000. Insurance costs are 0.1% of the new value of the airplane. The interest rate for discount purposes is 12%.

The spreadsheet answering the following questions should be well-organized and the various parts should be appropriately formatted. Data sections and range names should be used to enhance the presentation.

(a) Determine the net cash flow of this project and find its net present value and internal rate of return.

(b) Assume now that a loan can be used to finance 50% of the value of the airplane at an annual interest rate of 10%. Constant annual payments for the sum of interest and repayments are made over 20 years. Give the loan repayment scheme, the resulting net cash flow and its net present value and internal rate of return.

(c) Make separate bar graphs of the cash flow before loan, the loan cash flow and the cash flow after the loan, and name these FIG1, FIG2, and FIG3. Make a line graph including the three cash flows and name it FIG4. Use appropriate subcommands of the Options menu to enhance the graphic representation.

(d) Consider now a lease with monthly payments. Assuming that only the airplane purchase price must be covered, what is the monthly lease amount giving a return of 12%? What is this amount if also the overhaul and insurance costs and the residual value are taken into account?

(e) Using Data Table, find the monthly lease amount for returns 10%, 11%, … 20%.

(f) Now assume that leases with a term of 3 years are made with monthly payments, but that those payments should also include a change-over period of 6 months after the lease expires to allow for the time lost when the airplane cannot be leased out again immediately. What is the monthly lease amount in this case for a return of 12%?

(g) Use Data Table to find the monthly lease amount for terms varying from 3–10 years and change-over periods from 3–10 months.

Chapter 11
Evaluation of Resource Extraction Projects

Oil and gas projects have special terminology as well as structure, and both are introduced in this chapter. First the particulars of oil and gas production are explained and the structure of the revenues and costs is set out. An example of an oil prospect is given together with a spreadsheet-based economic evaluation. Sensitivity analysis by Data Table is used to find the consequences of varying production and oil price.

11.1 Oil and Gas Production

Oil and gas projects can be easily evaluated using net present values and internal rates of return because each project stands more or less on its own, with most of the costs at the start and the revenues coming from a limited number of years during which the reserves are produced. First a description is given of an oil and gas production project, then the various factors included in an evaluation are discussed, and finally the resulting spreadsheet is explained.

Because oil and gas are found underground, ownership of a piece of land may be subdivided into surface rights and mineral rights. The owners of the surface rights may also be owners of the mineral rights, but in Canada this is usually not so. The surface rights may be owned by private persons, but the mineral rights are usually owned by the Crown. Exceptions are Indian lands and certain pieces of land given out early. The mineral rights owned by the Crown have been transferred to the provinces, which lease these out for certain parcels for a certain period to oil and gas companies.

Leases of mineral rights are auctioned off to oil companies who have to submit closed bids. The bid, when accepted, is called *bonus*, and has to be paid in cash to the province, which will also receive part of the proceeds of production in the form of royalties.

Before bidding on any lease, the companies will try to obtain information about oil and gas prospects including seismic exploration and geological analysis.

After a company has submitted a winning bid on the mineral rights of a particular piece of land, it will drill an exploratory well. The depth of this well varies according to the geology. Let us assume it is 1600 m. Costs per meter may be about $200, so that the drilling costs are $320,000.

The result may be a dry hole, which means that no hydrocarbons are found or such small quantities that they are not commercially worthwhile. The well is then abandoned, and the costs made so far have resulted in no gain.

In the other case, oil may have been found, or gas, or both. The well must then be completed for production and connected to pipelines. Costs of this may vary according to location, but for a gas well it may easily be $200,000.

Then production may start, which may consist of more than one product, that is, the well may produce both oil and gas, while, furthermore, the gas may contain valuable gas liquids. Initially, the production is high and stays that way for one or more years, but then it declines. In many cases it is assumed that the production decline is exponential, which means that there is the same percentage decline every year. The production is assumed to stop when marginal operating costs exceed marginal revenues. In the latter case, the well has reached the end of its *economic life*.

11.2 Revenues and Costs

Oil and gas prospects are evaluated by taking expected revenues and subtracting from these expected costs and other related expenditures. Schematically:

Revenues
— Royalties
— Operating Costs
= Operating Profit
— Capital Investment
— Income Taxes
= After-Tax Cash Flow

To evaluate a project, prices for oil and gas have to be projected over the economic life of the well. It is obviously very difficult to forecast oil and gas prices. Currently the oil prices in Alberta are linked to world oil prices, which are volatile. Gas prices in Alberta are free, but those in British Columbia are regulated to a certain extent. The usual assumptions for oil and gas prices are to take the current prices for the present and assume that these are going to increase exponentially with a given percentage per year.

The multiplication of projected production and prices leads to projected *resource revenues*.

Out of these revenues the royalties have to be paid, which are a percentage of the revenues. Depending on the ownership of the mineral rights, these are Crown royalties if the mineral rights are owned by the province, or freehold royalties if they are owned by private persons or enterprises. Crown royalties may be fairly complicated functions of both production volumes and prices, and vary according to circumstances. In case of a freehold lease, a additional mineral tax has to be paid to the province, which is structured as a royalty.

If the company undertaking the project has taken over the lease from another party, they may have agreed to pay an *overriding royalty* to that party. Such an overriding royalty may be gross, in which case a percentage is taken from the resource revenues, or it may be net, in which case it is taken from the revenues net of the crown or freehold royalties. After all royalties have been subtracted from the resource revenues, the *revenue after royalties* results.

Now costs should be subtracted. In the first place there are the drilling and development and tie-in costs, discussed above, which are incurred at the start of the project. For each year of production there are fixed costs, which are the costs of keeping the well in production, for example $25,000 per year. Then there are variable costs, which are costs per unit produced, which may be pipeline costs and treatment costs for gas. These variable costs may easily be 10–20% of the price.

As all prices and costs go up over the years, a cost inflation percentage must be specified. All costs may be added to give *total costs*. Subtracting total costs from revenues after royalties, we obtain *cash flow before income tax*.

The project may be undertaken by just one company or by a number of partners who each have working interest which is expressed as a percentage. This means that each partner pays and gets this percentage of the cash flow before income tax. The evaluation takes place from the point of view of one partner with a given working interest percentage, so that the *own working interest* may be determined.

From this own working interest, federal and provincial taxes should be subtracted. Taxation varies with jurisdiction and is usually fairly complicated because of the rules regarding costs that may be subtracted from income. Royalties cannot be subtracted from income for income tax purposes, but to compensate for this, there is a royalty tax rebate for provincial income tax purposes and a 25% allowance for federal income tax purposes.

Cash flow after income tax can now be determined. In the last years of the project this cash flow may be negative. For years with a negative cash flow it is better to shut the project down, in which case the economic life is shorter than the project life. In this case oil or gas is left in the ground because the small production flows do not justify operating costs.

The resulting cash flow is the income stream which the company is evaluating. Three measures of performance based on this cash flow can be used:

1. Net Present Value at various interest rates.
2. The Internal Rate of Return.
3. The Payback or Payout period.

Note that this evaluation may not take into account sunk costs, such as the costs of obtaining the lease and seismic exploration. High present values and rates of return do therefore not necessarily indicate projects that are profitable on a full-cycle basis.

11.3 An Oil Prospect Evaluation

Let us consider the following oil prospect and evaluate it using the net present value at interest rates of 10%, 15%, and 20%, the internal rate of return, and the payback period.

It concerns a well that is being drilled in Year 0 at a cost of $1,500,000. It is expected to produce for 20 years or the economic life, beginning in Year 1, with 150 barrels per day, but the production declines by 10% per year. The Crown royalty is 25%, and there is an overriding royalty of 10%. The working interest in the well is 60%. In Year 0 variable costs of production are $5 per barrel. and fixed costs $100,000. Cost inflation is 5% per year. The initial oil price is $22, increasing at 6% per year. The federal tax rate is 30% and the provincial tax rate 15%.

Panel 11.1 contains these data in the data section and the results in the evaluation part. It is useful to give names to each of the data cells in C4 to C9 and G4 to G10, as indicated in the cells to the left of the data cells. The results for the various years are arranged columnwise and the items that make up the evaluation, rowwise. The reverse arrangement is also possible.

Production

The first row contains the annual production. In this case only one product, oil, is assumed, but usually there are multiple products, including gas and gas liquids. The initial daily production is given as 150 barrels per day, and the number of days in the year is 365, so that the annual production is 365*IDP. If leap years are taken into account, the number of days can be represented by

=IF(MOD(YEAR,4)=(,366,365)

where YEAR is the cell containing the year. For subsequent years the annual production is found by using the annual production decline factor AD.

Revenues

The oil price in Year 1 is given by OP and for the following years the annual oil price increase factor OPI should be used. Price times production results in Resource Revenue, see row 15. In case of multiple products the resource revenue for each product should be calculated.

Royalties

Crown and gross overriding royalties are usually a given percentage of the resource revenues. Subtracting these from the resource revenues gives the Revenues after Royalties, see row 18.

Operating Costs

Costs are distinguished in fixed costs that are time-related and variable costs that depend on production. In Year 0 drilling, development, and tie-in costs are incurred of $1,500,000, and in each production year, there are fixed production costs of $100,000 (in dollars of Year 0), starting in Year 1 and to be inflated with the cost inflation rate

Panel 11.1a Excel worksheet 1

	A	B	C	D	E	F	G	H	I	J
1	**Panel 1. Oilwell Evaluation.**									
2										
3	Data							Results		
4	Initial Daily Production	IDP	150	Drilling Costs		DC	$1,500,000		Disc.Int.R.	NPV
5	Annual Decline	AD	10%	Fixed Costs		FX	$100,000	Proj. Pr. Val.	10%	$271,023
6	Oil Price	OP	$22	Variable Costs		VC	$5		15%	$125,594
7	Oil Price Increase	OPI	6%	Cost Inflation		CI	5%		20%	$23,317
8	Crown Royalty	CR	25%	Working Interest		WI	60%	Internal Rate of Return		21.40%
9	Gross Overriding Royalty	GOR	10%	Federal Incoem Tax		FIT	30%	Payback Period		4
10				Provincial Income Tax		PIT	15%			
11	Evaluation									
12	Year	0	1	2	3	4	5	6	7	8
13	Annual Production		54750	49275	44348	39913	35921	32329	29096	26187
14	Price		$23.32	$24.72	$26.20	$27.77	$29.44	$31.21	$33.08	$35.06
15	Resource Revenue		$1,276,770	$1,218,039	$1,162,009	$1,108,556	$1,057,563	$1,008,915	$962,505	$918,230
16	Crown Royalty		$319,193	$304,510	$290,502	$277,139	$264,391	$252,229	$240,626	$229,557
17	Gross Overriding Royalty		$127,677	$121,804	$116,201	$110,856	$105,756	$100,891	$96,250	$91,823
18	Revenue after Royalties		$829,901	$791,725	$755,306	$720,562	$687,416	$655,795	$625,628	$596,849
19	Fixed Costs	$1,500,000	$105,000	$110,250	$115,763	$121,551	$127,628	$134,010	$140,710	$147,746
20	Variable Costs		$287,438	$271,628	$256,689	$242,571	$229,230	$216,622	$204,708	$193,449
21	Total Costs	$1,500,000	$392,438	$381,878	$372,451	$364,122	$356,858	$350,632	$345,418	$341,194
22	Cashflow before Income Tax	($1,500,000)	$437,463	$409,847	$382,854	$356,440	$330,558	$305,163	$280,210	$255,655
23	Working Interest	($900,000)	$262,478	$245,908	$229,713	$213,864	$198,335	$183,098	$168,126	$153,393
24	Federal Income Tax	($270,000)	$78,743	$73,772	$68,914	$64,159	$59,500	$54,929	$50,438	$46,018
25	Provincial Income Tax	($135,000)	$39,372	$36,886	$34,457	$32,080	$29,750	$27,465	$25,219	$23,009
26	Cashflow after Tax	($135,000)	$144,363	$135,249	$126,342	$117,625	$109,084	$100,704	$92,469	$84,366
27	Cashflow Economic Life	($495,000)	$144,363	$135,249	$126,342	$117,625	$109,084	$100,704	$92,469	$84,366
28	Discounted Cash Flow, 15%	($495,000)	$125,533	$102,268	$83,072	$67,253	$54,234	$43,537	$34,763	$27,579
29	Accumulated Cashflow	($495,000)	($350,637)	($215,388)	($89,046)	$28,579	$137,664	$238,367	$330,837	$415,203
30	Payback Period Calculation	1	1	1	1	0	0	0	0	0

Panel 11.1b Excel worksheet 2

Oilwell Evaluation, Continued.

Row	K	L	M	N	O	P	Q	R	S	T	U	V
	9	10	11	12	13	14	15	16	17	18	19	20
12	23568	21211	19090	17181	15463	13917	12525	11273	10145	9131	8218	7396
13	$37.17	$39.40	$41.76	$44.27	$46.92	$49.74	$52.72	$55.89	$59.24	$62.80	$66.56	$70.56
14	$875,991	$835,695	$797,253	$760,580	$725,593	$692,216	$660,374	$629,997	$601,017	$573,370	$546,995	$521,833
15	$218,998	$208,924	$199,313	$190,145	$181,398	$173,054	$165,093	$157,499	$150,254	$143,343	$136,749	$130,458
16	$87,599	$83,570	$79,725	$76,058	$72,559	$69,222	$66,037	$63,000	$60,102	$57,337	$54,700	$52,183
17	$569,394	$543,202	$518,215	$494,377	$471,636	$449,940	$429,243	$409,498	$390,661	$372,691	$355,547	$339,192
18	$155,133	$162,889	$171,034	$179,586	$188,565	$197,993	$207,893	$218,287	$229,202	$240,662	$252,695	$265,330
19	$182,809	$172,755	$163,253	$154,274	$145,789	$137,771	$130,193	$123,033	$116,266	$109,871	$103,828	$98,118
20	$337,942	$335,644	$334,287	$333,860	$334,354	$335,764	$338,086	$341,320	$345,468	$350,533	$356,523	$363,448
21	$231,452	$207,558	$183,928	$160,517	$137,281	$114,176	$91,157	$68,178	$45,193	$22,157	($977)	($24,256)
22	$138,871	$124,535	$110,357	$96,310	$82,369	$68,506	$54,694	$40,907	$27,116	$13,294	($586)	($14,554)
23	$41,661	$37,360	$33,107	$28,893	$24,711	$20,552	$16,408	$12,272	$8,135	$3,988	($176)	($4,365)
24	$20,831	$18,680	$16,553	$14,447	$12,355	$10,276	$8,204	$6,136	$4,067	$1,994	($88)	($2,183)
25	$76,379	$68,494	$60,696	$52,971	$45,303	$37,678	$30,082	$22,499	$14,914	$7,312	($322)	($8,004)
26	$76,379	$68,494	$60,696	$52,971	$45,303	$37,678	$30,082	$22,499	$14,914	$7,312	$0	$0
27	$21,712	$16,931	$13,046	$9,901	$7,363	$5,325	$3,697	$2,404	$1,386	$591	$0	$0
28	$491,582	$560,076	$620,772	$673,743	$719,046	$756,724	$786,806	$809,305	$824,218	$831,530	$831,530	$831,530
29	0	0	0	0	0	0	0	0	0	0	0	0

given by CI. Variable costs per units in Year 0 are VC. Total variable costs are found by multiplying the annual production by VC and the cost inflation factor. Fixed and variable costs are added to give Total Costs.

Before Tax Cash Flow

Total costs are subtracted from Revenue after Royalties to yield Cash Flow before Income Tax, see row 22. This is multiplied by the Working Interest factor WI to give the Working Interest cash flow before taxes.

After Tax Cash Flow

In this case it is assumed that for tax purposes all costs can be subtracted fully, as soon as they are made, from income from this project or from other income, and that they are a fixed percentage of income. This results in negative income taxes in Year 0, when the project does not yet give any income. Subtracting federal and provincial income tax results in Cash flow after Tax, see row 26.

In Year 19 this cash flow is negative, which means that production should be terminated. The economic life is therefore 18 years. Cash flow for Economic Life is 0 for the years 19 and 20.

Performance Measures

The Cash flow for Economic Life is used to determine the net present values, the internal rate of return, and the payback period. For the present values we have:

=NPV(DIR,C27:V27) +B27,

where DIR is the discount interest rate, and for the internal rate of return

=IRR(B27:V27,15%).

As the spreadsheet indicates, the internal rate of return is 21.4% and the present values range from $23,317 for a 20% discount rate to $271,026 for 10%.

To determine the pay-back period, first the accumulated cash flow is calculated, see row 29. The function

=IF(B29<1,0)

gives 1 for a negative cash flow, which is entered in row 30. The payback period in C36 is then simply the sum of the cells in row 30.

Panel 11.2 gives a column chart for the cash flow for economic life. It is obvious that, even without discounting, the revenues in the first few years are of importance.

Obviously the project evaluated in Panel 11.1 is a profitable one for the data given. There is, however, considerable uncertainty involved in many of the data. The oil price changes easily, the production decline factor may be different, royalties and taxes may change, costs may turn out to be underestimated, and so on. Sensitivity analysis with respect to all of these factors may give an idea of the amount of risk involved in this project.

Panel 11.2 Cash flow for Economic Life

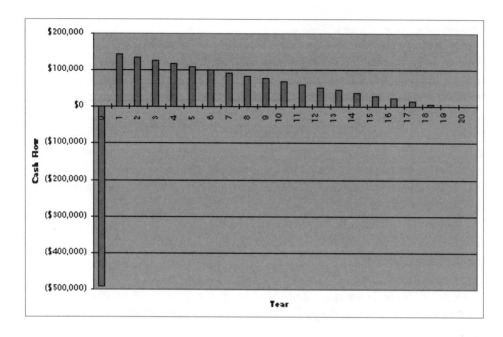

The **Data, Table** command can be used to find the net present values for varying oil price increases and initial production, see Panel 11.3. The formula of C33 is used together with the input cells OPI and IDP. Note that the project is very unprofitable for low values of both factors and very profitable for high values. Panel 11.4 gives a graphical display for varying oil price increases.

It should be noted that oil and gas prices are very volatile, so that the exponential increase of these prices is rather unrealistic. Production and production costs are also rather unpredictable (there may be a well blow-out with very high costs). It is possible to include the uncertainty in the model, but this requires probabilistic techniques and simulation.

Panel 11.3 Net Present Values for Varying Oil Price Increases and Initial Production

	F	G	H	I	J	K	L
36	$ 125,594	100	110	120	130	140	150
37	2%	($286,062)	($246,675)	($206,491)	($165,667)	($124,412)	($82,792)
38	3%	($263,221)	($219,910)	($176,037)	($131,197)	($86,149)	($40,503)
39	4%	($236,850)	($189,123)	($140,675)	($91,742)	($42,236)	$7,682
40	5%	($205,833)	($153,345)	($100,112)	($46,329)	$8,028	$62,757
41	6%	($169,837)	($111,904)	($53,241)	$5,976	$65,613	$125,594
42	7%	($127,858)	($63,850)	$818	$65,971	$131,456	$196,940
43	8%	($78,785)	($8,177)	$62,473	$133,123	$203,773	$274,423
44	9%	($23,046)	$53,182	$129,410	$205,638	$281,866	$358,094

Panel 11.4 Net Present Values for Varying Oil Price Increases

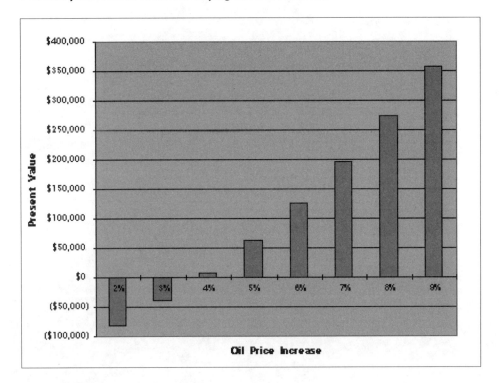

Exercises

11.1. Assume that the $1,500,000 costs in Year 0 cannot be subtracted from income in that year, but that these costs are equally distributed over the 18 years of economic life, and are subtracted from income in these years. How does this change the results of the evaluation?

11.2. Using the Data, Table command, perform sensitivity analysis of the present values and the internal rate of return with respect to changes in Crown royalty and federal and provincial income taxes.

11.3. Find in a database or elsewhere oil prices and price index numbers for the years 1970 to the present. Assume that the oil well is drilled in 1970 instead of in Year 0. Adjust the oil price and costs using the oil prices and the index numbers. Assume that the 6% oil price increase and the 5% cost inflation were used in 1970 to evaluate the oil well prospect, and give the resulting net present values and the corresponding internal rate of return. Now, instead of the oil price and cost inflation projections use the historic data and find the resulting net present values and internal rate of return. Compare these with the ones found earlier.

   Perform the same comparison for other years, assuming that oil prices and costs beyond the present will follow the projections.

part 4

Database Management Applications

Chapter 12
Basic Database Tools

This chapter discusses the handling of a database by means of editing, sorting and filtering.

In this chapter you will learn the following spreadsheet commands and functions:

- Data Form
- Sort Ascending, Descending
- Data Sort
- Data Filter

12.1 Introduction

Spreadsheets are useful for storing, manipulating, and analyzing business and other data. In many cases the quantity of data generated and used is large, which makes their use more cumbersome. Data of a size of one or a few screens can easily be scanned and what is needed can be done by 'manual' selection and handling, but if the amount is larger, this becomes more difficult, time-consuming, and error prone. For this reason a number of tools for handling data have been included in the spreadsheet system.

Data can only be used in an efficient manner if it is systematically arranged. Such an arrangement is usually in terms of rectangular arrays or blocs, each of which may be called a *database*, or a *list*.

A database consists of a number of *records*, displayed in rows, each having entries for a number of *fields*, displayed in columns. Panel 12.1 gives an example of a customer database containing the customer number, name, credit class, orders 1998 and 1997,

Panel 12.1 Example of a Database

	A	B	C	D	E	F
1	DATA					
2	No	Name	Credit	Orders 1998	Orders 1997	Outst. Credit
3	2	Hadwick & Gross	A	$ 27,327	$ 36,078	$ 7,854
4	5	Fairplay	D	$ 66,906	$ -	$ 300
5	8	Grimby & Co	B	$ 20,756	$ 26,746	$ 3,450
6	10	Fisher Inc.	A	$ 80,679	$ 75,408	$ 2,103
7	12	Van der Straaten	B	$ 49,516	$ 42,093	$ 3,394
8	14	McAdams	C	$ 58,010	$ 52,406	$ 145
9	17	Morningseed Inc	C	$ 6,440	$ 15,028	$ 1,547
10	23	Northern Star	A	$ 84,323	$ 76,186	$ 4,100
11	24	Dybuk Brothers	B	$ 46,032	$ 37,691	$ 5,260
12	32	Hu & Wong	A	$ 80,684	$ 67,931	$ 6,608

and outstanding credit for each customer, see row 2 in Panel 12.1, which gives the field names of the database.

Since databases are large, it is useful, in order to avoid having to find their ranges, to give names. In Panel 12.1, the range A2:F12 has been given the name DATA, which, for ease of recognition, has been entered above the range.

Generally, the area to the right of the database should be left empty, because nonblank cells may be affected by manipulations involving rows of the database.

12.2 Data Form: A Database Editing Tool

As databases tend to be large, editing can be difficult. If a record is to be deleted, it has to be found, selected, and deleted, after which the free space has to be filled up. The latter can be done by deleting the row, but only if that row does not contain any other nonblank cells. Furthermore, we may wish to have a close look at each of the individual data cells, in order to check the data, which may not be easy in a screen full of similar cells.

The command **Data, Form** facilitates such editing and checking. First the database including field names is selected. After the command is activated, the first record is displayed such as that given in Panel 12.2.

Panel 12.2 The Data Form Display of a Record

It has a number of useful features:

1. Only one record is displayed at the same time.

2. Only original data (numbers or text) are displayed, cells with formulas do not have a field.

3. A record may be deleted permanently by means of the 'Delete' button, which automatically deletes the open space in the database.

4. New records may be added by means of the 'New' button, which allows the data of the new record to be entered.

5. Movement to other records is by means of the 'Find Next' and 'Find Prev' buttons or, for more distant records, via the scroll bar.

6. The 'Criteria' button makes it possible to enter criteria in a field, after which only records satisfying these are displayed. Entering 'A' in the credit field results in records all having that credit class, and >50000 in the orders 1998 field limits the records to those meeting that condition.

12.3 Sorting Data

If a single column of numbers or text must be sorted, this can be done by selection of the range and then clicking on one of the sort buttons of the tools bar, see top of Panel 12.3. The left-hand button sorts in ascending order and the right-hand one in the opposite direction. If multiple columns are involved, the **Data, Sort** command should be used.

Suppose the customers and their data need to be sorted alphabetically. This is done by selection of the data range A3:F12 and then invoking the **Data, Sort** command which displays the control menu given in Panel 12.3. The *Sort* by pull-down tab is used to select the *Name* column for sorting. Note that the system automatically lists the field names. For alphabetical sorting, the *Ascending* option should be chosen. The result is found in Panel 12.4.

Immediately after the command has been executed, it can be reversed via the command **Edit, Undo**. After any further change this is no longer possible, so that the initial sequence of the data could be lost, which sometimes is not desirable. To avoid this, the records can be numbered, so that the data in their original order may be restored.

For the sorting of character (label or text) data, digits come before letters. For other symbols, see **Excel Help, Sort Default Order**.

It is also possible to sort by numerical field, such as Orders in 1998, with the customers having the largest order amount coming first, so that the sort order is descending. The result is given in Panel 12.5.

Panel 12.3 Sort Buttons and Menu for Sort by Name

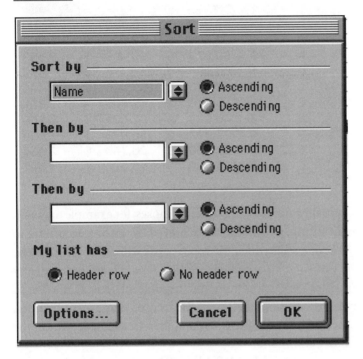

Panel 12.4 The Result of Sorting by Character Field

	A	B	C	D	E	F
1	DATA					
2	No	Name	Credit	Orders 1998	Orders 1997	Outst. Credit
3	24	Dybuk Brothers	B	$ 46,032	$ 37,691	$ 5,260
4	5	Fairplay	D	$ 66,906	$ -	$ 300
5	10	Fisher Inc.	A	$ 80,679	$ 75,408	$ 2,103
6	8	Grimby & Co	B	$ 20,756	$ 26,746	$ 3,450
7	2	Hadwick & Gross	A	$ 27,327	$ 36,078	$ 7,854
8	32	Hu & Wong	A	$ 80,684	$ 67,931	$ 6,608
9	14	McAdams	C	$ 58,010	$ 52,406	$ 145
10	17	Morningseed Inc	C	$ 6,440	$ 15,028	$ 1,547
11	23	Northern Star	A	$ 84,323	$ 76,186	$ 4,100
12	12	Van der Straaten	B	$ 49,516	$ 42,093	$ 3,394

Panel 12.5 The Result of Sorting by Order Amount

	A	B	C	D	E	F
1	DATA					
2	No	Name	Credit	Orders 1998	Orders 1997	Outst. Credit
3	23	Northern Star	A	$ 84,323	$ 76,186	$ 4,100
4	32	Hu & Wong	A	$ 80,684	$ 67,931	$ 6,608
5	10	Fisher Inc.	A	$ 80,679	$ 75,408	$ 2,103
6	5	Fairplay	D	$ 66,906	$ -	$ 300
7	14	McAdams	C	$ 58,010	$ 52,406	$ 145
8	12	Van der Straaten	B	$ 49,516	$ 42,093	$ 3,394
9	24	Dybuk Brothers	B	$ 46,032	$ 37,691	$ 5,260
10	2	Hadwick & Gross	A	$ 27,327	$ 36,078	$ 7,854
11	8	Grimby & Co	B	$ 20,756	$ 26,746	$ 3,450
12	17	Morningseed Inc	C	$ 6,440	$ 15,028	$ 1,547

Sorting can be used as a preliminary step for other purposes, for example to obtain all records with a low credit rating, which may be achieved by sorting according to credit rating in descending order, after which the top records with a D rating may be selected. The disadvantages of such an approach are that the data are permanently altered, which may be undesirable. Furthermore, the number of records may be so large that the selection and further manipulation of the records may give difficulties. For these reasons many other tools for dealing with databases are available. One of the simpler tools is the **Data, Filter** command.

In most cases, databases are organized with fields in columns and records in rows. In the rare instances with the reverse arrangements, the sorting orientation can be reversed by means of the 'Options' button in the sort menu, where the 'Sort Left to Right' option can be selected.

This feature can be used if the order of fields in a database should be changed. This is done by entering over the field names numbers indicating the desired order of the fields. A selection of the database including these numbers allows a sorting from left to right with the desired results.

12.4 Filtering Records

Sorting is relatively uncomplicated because it is easy to indicate what should be done, since sorting can only be done according to one or two columns, in an either ascending or descending direction. For extracting, deleting, and finding records more detailed criteria are needed. These operations can be implemented by means of the **Data, Filter** command.

For an explanation of the **Filter** subcommand, assume that we want to extract the records of customers with an A credit rating, see Panel 12.6. First the records plus field names involved are selected, then the **Data, Filter, AutoFilter** command is invoked.

This results in drop-down menus being displayed. Clicking and holding on the Credit. tab, the entries given in Panel 12.6 are displayed. After selection of A, only customers with an A credit rating are displayed, see Panel 12.7.

Panel 12.6 Filtering Data

	A	B	C	D	E	F
1	DATA					
2		Name	(All)		Orders 199	Outst. Cred
3	2	Hadwick & Gross	(Top 10...)		$ 36,078	$ 7,854
4	5	Fairplay	(Custom...)		$ -	$ 300
5	8	Grimby & Co	A		$ 26,746	$ 3,450
6	10	Fisher Inc.	B		$ 75,408	$ 2,103
7	12	Van der Straaten	C		$ 42,093	$ 3,394
8	14	McAdams	D		$ 52,406	$ 145
9	17	Morningseed Inc	C	$ 6,440	$ 15,028	$ 1,547
10	23	Northern Star	A	$ 84,323	$ 76,186	$ 4,100
11	24	Dybuk Brothers	B	$ 46,032	$ 37,691	$ 5,260
12	32	Hu & Wong	A	$ 80,684	$ 67,931	$ 6,608

Panel 12.7 The Filtered Result

	A	B	C	D	E	F
1	DATA					
2		Name	Cred	Orders 199	Orders 199	Outst. Cred
3	2	Hadwick & Gross	A	$ 27,327	$ 36,078	$ 7,854
6	10	Fisher Inc.	A	$ 80,679	$ 75,408	$ 2,103
10	23	Northern Star	A	$ 84,323	$ 76,186	$ 4,100
12	32	Hu & Wong	A	$ 80,684	$ 67,931	$ 6,608

In the result, only the records of customers with an A credit rating are displayed. The other records are temporarily hidden. They can be made visible again by the command **Data, Filter, Show All**. Note that the row numbers of the selected records are blue, as well as the tab of the field used in the selection.

The range of the selected records may be copied to another place, or used to obtain sums and averages. Note that, unlike the Sort command, the Filter command does not change the original database.

The previous situation is recovered by invoking the subcommand Show All and turning off AutoFilter.

Suppose that, of all customers with an A credit rating only these with orders in 1998 of at least $50,000 are required. The corresponding tab in column D is then selected, and dragged to 'custom', after which the menu displayed in Panel 12.8 appears.

Panel 12.8 The Custom AutoFilter Menu

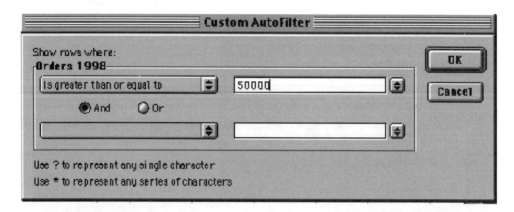

The left drop-down list is used to select 'is greater than or equal to' criterion and 50000 is entered in the first numerical field. The right-hand drop-down list gives access to each of the numbers in the Orders 1998 column. The result is given in Panel 12.9.

Panel 12.9 The Result with Two Filter Settings

	A	B	C	D	E	F
1	DATA					
2		Name	Cred	Orders 199	Orders 199	Outst. Cre
4	5	Fairplay	D	$ 66,906	$ -	$ 300
6	10	Fisher Inc.	A	$ 80,679	$ 75,408	$ 2,103
8	14	McAdams	C	$ 58,010	$ 52,406	$ 145
10	23	Northern Star	A	$ 84,323	$ 76,186	$ 4,100
12	32	Hu & Wong	A	$ 80,684	$ 67,931	$ 6,608

12.5 Criteria Range and Advanced Filter

It is also possible to use the subcommand of **Data, Filter, Advanced Filter**, which works in the same way except that the records are not selected via the drop-down lists but with a criteria range. Suppose the same selection as in Panel 12.9 is required, with the credit rating of A and 1998 orders over $50,000. The criteria range consists of the field names with below these the conditions put on the records, see Panel 12.10.

Panel 12.10 The Criteria Range

	H	I
10	Credit	Orders 1998
11	A	>50000

After the Advanced Filter command is invoked, the corresponding menu appears, see Panel 12.11. The number field must be filled. Completion of the command gives Panel 12.12, which is identical to Panel 12.9, except for the drop-down lists.

Panel 12.11 Advanced Filter Menu

Panel 12.12 The Result of Advanced Filter

	A	B	C	D	E	F
1	DATA					
2	No Name		Credit	Orders 1998	Orders 1997	Outst. Credit
6	10 Fisher Inc.		A	$ 80,679	$ 75,408	$ 2,103
10	23 Northern Star		A	$ 84,323	$ 76,186	$ 4,100
12	32 Hu & Wong		A	$ 80,684	$ 67,931	$ 6,608

In the above example the same results were obtained with AutoFilter. The criteria range, however, makes it possible to filter with more complicated conditions. Suppose that all records with credit class A or with 1998 orders larger than 50,000 are required. The AutoFilter command cannot handle this request, but the Advanced Filter can. For the 'or' conditions (indicated by selecting 'or' and then completing the drop-down lists in menus in the AutoFilter menu, see Panel 12.8) the criteria range contains a different row, so that this range is now as given in Panel 12.13.

Panel 12.13 The Criteria Range for 'or' Conditions

	H	I
10	Credit	Orders 1998
11	A	
12		>50000

The result is given in Panel 12.14. There are six records satisfying the conditions, whereas for the 'and' conditions there were only three. The same criteria ranges will later be used in database statistical functions.

Panel 12.14 The Result for 'or' Conditions

	A	B	C	D	E	F
1	DATA					
2	No	Name	Credit	Orders 1998	Orders 1997	Outst. Credit
3	2	Hadwick & Gross	A	$ 27,327	$ 36,078	$ 7,854
4	5	Fairplay	D	$ 66,906	$ -	$ 300
6	10	Fisher Inc.	A	$ 80,679	$ 75,408	$ 2,103
8	14	McAdams	C	$ 58,010	$ 52,406	$ 145
10	23	Northern Star	A	$ 84,323	$ 76,186	$ 4,100
12	32	Hu & Wong	A	$ 80,684	$ 67,931	$ 6,608

Exercises

12.1 Sort the data according to Orders in 1998 and build a column chart for the customer orders in 1998 and 1997.

12.2 With the Data Sort command rearrange the database of Panel 12.1 with fields in the following order: Name, No, Orders 1998, Orders 1997, Outst. Credit, Credit.

12.3 Determine for each customer the outstanding credit as a percentage of 1998 orders and find out whether the average percentages differ for different credit classes.

Assignment

12.1 Real Estate Database

On the disk accompanying this book is the database in the sheet C1DATA, which is concerned with real estate properties.

(a) Use the Data, Form command with criteria to select the properties that are in the North-West, have at least 2,000 sq. ft, have been built later than 1980, and with a price < $300,000. How many properties did you find?

(b) Use the Data, Sort command to obtain the same result.

(c) Use the Data, Filter, AutoFilter command to do the same.

(d) Use the Advanced Filter command with criteria range to obtain the results.

(e) Using the Data, Sort command, rearrange the fields such that the price becomes the second field.

Chapter 13
Looking up Data

This chapter discusses the handling of a database by means of lookup functions. It is also concerned with the construction of price discount schemes and general piecewise linear functions. It is shown that the income tax scheme can be represented as a piecewise linear function using a lookup table.

In this chapter you will learn the following spreadsheet commands and functions:

- Paste Function
- VLOOKUP(*cell,table,column number, range lookup*)
- HLOOKUP(*cell,table,column number, range lookup*)

13.1 The Paste Function Menu

Spreadsheets contain a large number of built-in functions. Of these, the function SUM has been introduced. Since this function is a very simple one, it needed little explanation. The operation of other functions is less obvious, for which reason the Excel spreadsheet contains the **Paste Function** menu, which is found on the standard toolbar as f_x. This feature guides the user through the steps required for the implementation of any selected function.

The **Paste Function** menu is activated by clicking on the f_x button on the tool, which results in the menu of Panel 13.1. The left-hand side displays the function category, of which any can be selected. The right hand-side shows the functions in that category. For example, the function SUM belongs to the Math & Trig category, so that it can be found by selecting this group. After SUM is selected in the right-hand side, its arguments are given, which usually is just one range of cells, but which for SUM may also be a number of separate cells or ranges or numbers, separated by a comma. A one-line definition of the function follows. The **Help** button (bottom left in Panel 13.1) leads to a more extensive explanation.

The OK button gives a menu for entering the function's arguments (see Panel 13.2), e.g. the numbers themselves; cell references of the cells that hold those numbers; a name of a cell or group of cells; the result of another function. In the field for Number 1, the range of cells to be added should be entered, either by means of the keyboard, or more conveniently, by using the mouse. In the field for Number 2 and other similar fields that may appear, additional ranges to be included in the function can be added.

Assume that we wish to find the total order amount over the years 1997 and 1998, see Panel 13.3. The range D3:D12 for the orders in 1998 is entered in the number 1 field and the range E3:E12 for 1997 in the Number 2 field of the Argument menu. The resulting value, $950,240, is displayed at the bottom of the menu. The function is completed by clicking the OK button, after which the formula is displayed in the

Panel 13.1 The Paste Function Menu

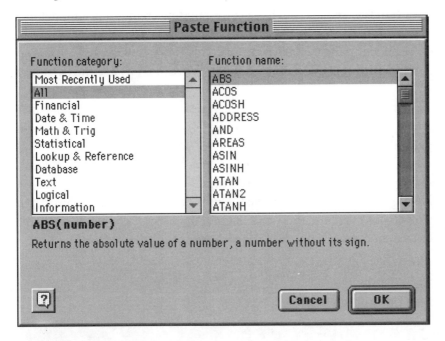

Panel 13.2 Argument Menu

selected cell. Its value is shown after completion by hitting the Return key or clicking the check mark on the control bar.

Any function including its arguments can be entered directly into a cell, without the help of the Paste Function command. This menu is convenient when a function is used for the first time or when one is not sure about some detail such as the order of the arguments. In other cases, it is usually more efficient to enter functions directly.

The most recently used functions are included in a drop-down list that appears to the left of the control bar after an equal sign (=) has been entered. The 'Other Functions' item gives access to the Paste Function menu.

13.2 The VLOOKUP Function

Suppose that each of the credit classes has a corresponding credit limit, and that this limit is for class A, $10,000, for B, $5,000, for C, $2,000, and for D, $0. These credit limits should be added to the customer records. This is done by means of a *lookup function* which looks up the credit class, for example B, in a lookup table and enters the result.

Lookup functions can be interpreted as the reverse of Data Tables. Data Tables construct arrays from single expressions, while lookup functions give a single expression derived from an array.

Two kinds of lookups can be distinguished: *exact* lookups and *range* lookups. Exact lookups are simpler and will be dealt with first.

First a lookup table must be constructed. This is done in the range A15:B18, see Panel 13.3. For ease of reference, this range is given the name CLT (for Credit Limit Table), which is entered above it. In cell G3, the following formula is entered:

=VLOOKUP(C3,CLT,2,0).

Panel 13.3 Credit Limit Lookup

	A	B	C	D	E	F	G
1	DATA						
2	No Name		Credit	Orders 1998	Orders 1997	Outst. Credit	Credit Limit
3	24 Dybuk Brothers	B	$	46,032	$ 37,691	$ 5,260	$ 5,000
4	5 Fairplay	D	$	66,906	$ -	$ 300	$ -
5	10 Fisher Inc.	A	$	80,679	$ 75,408	$ 2,103	$ 10,000
6	8 Grimby & Co	B	$	20,756	$ 26,746	$ 3,450	$ 5,000
7	2 Hadwick & Gross	A	$	27,327	$ 36,078	$ 7,854	$ 10,000
8	32 Hu & Wong	A	$	80,684	$ 67,931	$ 6,608	$ 10,000
9	14 McAdams	C	$	58,010	$ 52,406	$ 145	$ 2,000
10	17 Morningseed Inc	C	$	6,440	$ 15,028	$ 1,547	$ 2,000
11	23 Northern Star	A	$	84,323	$ 76,186	$ 4,100	$ 10,000
12	12 Van der Straaten	B	$	49,516	$ 42,093	$ 3,394	$ 5,000
13							
14	CLT						
15	A	$ 10,000					
16	B	$ 5,000					
17	C	$ 2,000					
18	D	$ -					

The function VLOOKUP has four arguments. The first one is *what* should be looked up, or the lookup value, which is, in this case, the credit class A in cell C3.

The second argument is *where* it should be looked up, namely in the lookup table or table array, here the range CLT. The lookup value should be looked up in the *first column* of CLT.

The third argument is the *column number* for the credit limit in that table. The credit rating occurs in column 2 of CLT, so that 2 is used.

The last argument indicates whether there should be an *exact lookup*, when the argument is 0 or FALSE, or whether it should be a *range* lookup, in which case it is 1 or TRUE, the default. In the current case the lookup should be exact, so that the argument is 0. If the argument is omitted, the default value of 1 is assumed, which in this case leads to unintended results (try it out!). The range lookup is explained later.

Instead of entering the function directly, the Paste Function command may be used. The selection of the VLOOKUP function leads to the menu displayed in Panel 13.4, in which the various fields have been filled out.

The remaining G-column cells are copied from G3.

Panel 13.4 The Menu for the VLOOKUP Function

13.3 Looking Up Database Information

Lookup functions can also be used to extract information from large databases. Assume that we have available the customer's number and that the corresponding credit rating is required. After entering in A23 the customer number 24 and in cell B23 the formula:

=VLOOKUP($A23,DB,3,0),

the credit rating B is obtained, see Panel 13.5.

This can be extended for looking up a number of entries of the same record, which is illustrated in the lower part of Panel 13.5. The values of the first argument of the lookup function, which indicate the lookup value, are entered in A26:A28, and the values of the third argument, the column number, are entered in the range B25:G25. These are used in the lookup function entered in cell B26:

=VLOOKUP($A26,DATA,B25,0).

Panel 13.5 Lookup of Database Records

	A	B	C	D	E	F	G
1	DATA						
2	No Name		Credit	Orders 1998	Orders 1997	Outst. Credit	Credit Limit
3	24 Dybuk Brothers	B	$	46,032	$ 37,691	$ 5,260	$ 5,000
4	5 Fairplay	D	$	66,906	$ -	$ 300	$ -
23	24 B						
24							
25		2	3	4	5	6	7
26	24 Dybuk Brothers	B	$	46,032	$ 37,691	$ 5,260	$ 5,000
27	10 Fisher Inc.	A	$	80,679	$ 75,408	$ 2,103	$ 10,000
28	5 Fairplay	D	$	66,906	$ -	$ 300	$ -
29							

This formula is then copied to the range B26:G28, which results in the desired parts of the selected records.

Further records can be generated by entering its number in column A, after which the cells in the columns B–G are copied from above. It is also possible to give cell B26 the formula:

=IF($A26="","",VLOOKUP($A26,DATA,B$25,0)).

If cell A26 is empty (" "), this results in an empty cell, if not, and A26 contains a customer number, the second field in the database for that customer results. This may be copied to the columns B - G and down a number of rows. Then by entering customer numbers in the column A, the parts of the corresponding records will appear.

13.4 A Lookup for a Pricing Schedule

In an exact lookup the lookup value must match exactly one of the cells in the first column of the lookup table. In range lookups, such an exact correspondence is not needed. In these lookups the cells to be looked up contain almost always values which should be looked up in a table consisting of ranges of values.

As an example, a schedule for quantity discounts of prices is considered, see Panel 13.6. For less than 10 units the price per unit is $0.50, for at least 10 but less than 50 units, the price is $0.45, for 50 to less than 100 it is $0.40, and so on, as illustrated in Panel 13.6. A price for a given quantity can be found by a lookup function based on the price table (C5:D9), which is named PRICES. Based on this, prices for quantities in intervals of 20 can be constructed in the range B2:B12. Cell B2 is given the formula:

=VLOOKUP(A2,PRICES,2,1).

Note that the fourth argument indicates that is is a range lookup, which might have been omitted because it is the default.

The lookup function will go to the first column of PRICES and move downwards until it finds a value that is higher. Then it will go back up one row, and read off in that

Panel 13.6 A Range Lookup for Prices

	A	B	C	D
1	No of Units	Price		
2	0	$ 0.50	<--=VLOOKUP(A2,PRICES,2)	
3	20	$ 0.45		
4	40	$ 0.45	PRICES	
5	60	$ 0.40	0	$ 0.50
6	80	$ 0.40	10	$ 0.45
7	100	$ 0.38	50	$ 0.40
8	120	$ 0.38	100	$ 0.38
9	140	$ 0.38	200	$ 0.36
10	160	$ 0.38		
11	180	$ 0.38		
12	200	$ 0.36		

row the cell in the required column. For the 0 in A2, the result is $0.50. Cell B2 is copied downwards, which gives the desired results.

A range lookup requires that the first column of the lookup table has an *ascending* order, since otherwise the results will make no sense (see the above description of the operation of the lookup function). This ascending order can easily be obtained by means of the **Data**, **Sort** command.

In a range lookup, both the lookup value and the first column of the lookup table may also contain character data. The implied order of characters is of course alphabetic, and values will precede characters. This may be of some use when names are divided alphabetically in a number of groups which will be given different attributes.

The function VLOOKUP is called the *vertical* lookup function, because the lookup table is organized in terms of columns. The function HLOOKUP works in the same way, except that the lookup table consist of rows, with the first row being used for the lookup value, while the third argument refers to the desired row of the table.

Another function called LOOKUP is available which handles more complicated situations.

13.5 Piecewise Linear Functions and Income Tax

The range lookup function can be used to build general piecewise linear functions such as given in the line chart of Panel 13.7. Each piece of line is determined by its intercept and its slope. These are given in the lookup table PRICE of Panel 13.7. The formula in cell B2 is then:

=VLOOKUP(A2,PRICE,2)+A2*VLOOKUP(A2,PRICE,3).

Note that intercepts and slopes must be related in a certain way to make the piecewise linear curve continuous.

Panel 13.7 Piecewise Linear Function

	A	B	C	D	E	F	G	H	I
1	No of Units	Price							
2	0	$ -		<--=VLOOKUP(A2,PRICE,2)+A2*VLOOKUP(A2,PRICE,3)					
3	5	$ 3.00							
4	10	$ 6.00							
5	15	$ 8.00							
6	20	$ 10.00							
7	25	$ 11.50							
8	30	$ 13.00							
9	35	$ 14.25							
10	40	$ 15.50							
11									
12									
13									
14	PRICE	Interc.	Slope						
15	0.0	$ -	0.60						
16	10.0	$ 2.00	0.40						
17	20.0	$ 4.00	0.30						
18	30.0	$ 5.50	0.25						

The same kind of curve is found in income tax calculations. The Canadian federal income tax schedule is that the tax of taxable incomes up to $28,784 is 17% of taxable income, for taxable incomes from $28,784–$ 57,568 the tax is $4,893 plus 26% of the difference between taxable income and $28,784, while for incomes above $57,568 the tax is $12,377 plus 29% of the difference of taxable income and $57,568.

The rates and values are given in Panel 13.8 in the range C2:E4, named TT. The income tax in B2 for a taxable income of A2 is then, following the description given above:

=VLOOKUP(A2,TT,2,1)+(A2-VLOOKUP(A2,TT,1,1))*VLOOKUP(A2,TT,3,1).

Panel 13.8 Federal Income Tax

	A	B	C	D	E
1	Income	Fed. Inc. Tax TT		Fixed amount	Percentage
2	$ -	$ -	$ -	$ -	17%
3	$ 10,000	$ 1,700	$ 28,784	$ 4,893	26%
4	$ 20,000	$ 3,400	$ 57,568	$ 12,377	29%
5	$ 30,000	$ 5,209			
6	$ 40,000	$ 7,809			
7	$ 50,000	$ 10,409			
8	$ 60,000	$ 13,082			
9	$ 70,000	$ 15,982			
10	$ 80,000	$ 18,882			
11	$ 90,000	$ 21,782			
12	$ 100,000	$ 24,682			

An alternative formulation using intercepts and slopes as indicated in Panel 13.7 is possible.

Panel 13.9 gives the relationship between income and federal tax, based on the range A2:B11. It is a line chart (and not a scatter graph), which works in this case because the numbers on the X-axis are equidistant.

Panel 13.9 Income and Federal Income Tax

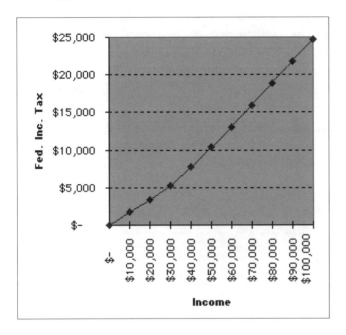

Exercises

13.1. Determine the total cost (= p*q) curve for the example of Panel 13.6. Comment on its shape.

13.2. Suppose that the amount of income tax depends on income and the state or province of residence. Construct a lookup function based on income and state or province of residence.

13.3. Convert the formulation of the lookup table of Panel 13.7 into that of Panel 13.8 and vice versa.

Assignments

13.1 The Student Record Case I

Given is the sheet C1DATA on the accompanying disk with class records for 100 students.

(a) Using a lookup table, convert the letter grades to numerical grades, using $A = 4, A- = 3.7, B+ = 3.3, B = 3, .., D = 1, F = 0$.

(b) Determine the average over all assignments for each student.

(c) Using a lookup table, convert these averages back into letter grades.

Chapter 14
Frequencies and Quantiles

This chapter discusses applications of frequency distributions and lookup functions to customer responses. First, the construction of frequency distributions for numerical data is discussed, after which two functions for ranking data are explained. Then the determination of the median, and other quantiles of a distribution are treated. The allocation of customers to percentage-based groups is outlined. Finally, value frequency distributions are extended to frequency distributions for labels.

In this chapter you will learn the following spreadsheet commands and functions:

- Add-Ins
- Data Analysis
- COUNT(*range*), COUNTA(*range*)
- Histogram
- FREQUENCY(*input range, bin range*)
- Edit Fill
- RANK(*number, range*)
- PERCENTRANK(*range, number*)
- MEDIAN(*range*)
- QUARTILE(*range, quarter*)
- PERCENTILE(*range,percent*)

14.1 Frequency Distributions for Values

The obvious questions to be asked of a database are: How many records are there and how many of different groups? This chapter discusses some commands and functions that provide answers to these questions.

As an example, a customer satisfaction report for a certain software is used, see Panel 14.1. This report gives the customer's number, name, location quadrant of the city, or out of town, and their satisfaction with the product as percentages.

The number of records in a database can be determined by the row numbers, but it is easier to use the function COUNTA which counts the number of nonblank cells in a certain range. Thus, in this case, by choosing the range of cells in column A and using the function COUNTA the number of records is:

=COUNTA(A2:A19)

which results in a count of 18.

The related function COUNT(range) gives the number of numeric cells in a range. The two functions can be differentiated by noting that the A in COUNTA could signify 'all'.

Panel 14.1 Customer Satisfaction Report

	A	B	C	D
1	No.	Customer	Location	Satisfaction
2	1	Macleod	SW	63.4%
3	3	Varsity	NE	86.4%
4	4	LowCost	NE	60.1%
5	6	Southridge	OT	70.3%
6	7	Restorator	SE	69.5%
7	9	Apple	SW	54.3%
8	12	Alpine	SW	75.1%
9	13	Precision	OT	50.8%
10	15	Ronaks	NW	62.7%
11	16	Universal	SE	30.4%
12	19	Phoenix	SW	69.5%
13	20	Horton	SW	65.5%
14	21	Shaw	NW	70.9%
15	24	Stampede	OT	55.9%
16	25	Elite	SE	91.4%
17	27	Espinola	OT	70.5%
18	28	Cosmos	SW	68.3%
19	29	Felix	SE	69.2%

Questions which might need to be answered in regard to this database are: How many customers are there in the various locations, and how many have satisfactions in the 90s, in the 80s, and so on. The first question requires a frequency distribution according to location, which is given by a *label* (character or text), and the second, a frequency distribution by *values* or numbers. In the following section, the value frequency distribution tools will be explained. Then it is demonstrated that a label frequency distribution can be obtained by means of a value frequency distribution.

14.1.1 Bin Range

A simple way to characterize the variation of numerical data is by a frequency distribution, which defines groups with lower and upper bounds and determines how many of the data are in any of the groups. Let us make a frequency distribution of the satisfaction percentages for the 18 customers, see Panel 14.2. First suitable limits must be chosen. Usually the best choice of limits is such that the resulting frequencies are not wildly different. In this case, limits at 10% intervals are taken.

In the spreadsheet these limits are indicated in the *bin range*, which gives these limits in a column, see range F2:F12 in Panel 14.2. *The bin range should always be in ascending order*. The headings in row 1 are added for clarification. The bin range has been given the percentage format, which, of course, does not affect its values.

The spreadsheet will enter next to each bin range cell the number of customers whose satisfaction does not exceed the number in that cell, but is larger than the previous number in the bin range, if there is one. In general, an item belongs to a group if it exceeds the lower bound l, but is at most equal to the upper bound u: $l < x \leq u$. The frequency is entered next to each upper bound u.

Panel 14.2 Frequency Distribution of Satisfaction

	A	B	C	D	E	F	G	H
1	No.	Customer	Location	Satisfaction		Bin Range	Bin	Frequency
2	1	Macleod	SW	63.4%		0%	0%	0
3	3	Varsity	NE	86.4%		10%	10%	0
4	4	LowCost	NE	60.1%		20%	20%	0
5	6	Southridge	OT	70.3%		30%	30%	0
6	7	Restorator	SE	69.5%		40%	40%	1
7	9	Apple	SW	54.3%		50%	50%	0
8	12	Alpine	SW	75.1%		60%	60%	3
9	13	Precision	OT	50.8%		70%	70%	8
10	15	Ronaks	NW	62.7%		80%	80%	4
11	16	Universal	SE	30.4%		90%	90%	1
12	19	Phoenix	SW	69.5%		100%	100%	1
13	20	Horton	SW	65.5%			More	0
14	21	Shaw	NW	70.9%				
15	24	Stampede	OT	55.9%				
16	25	Elite	SE	91.4%				
17	27	Espinola	OT	70.5%				
18	28	Cosmos	SW	68.3%				
19	29	Felix	SE	69.2%				

There are two alternative ways of obtaining the frequency distribution of numerical data, one is via the add-in **Histogram**, the other via the function FREQUENCY. Each has advantages and disadvantages.

14.1.2 The Histogram Add-In

Normally, the last subcommand of the **Tools** menu is **Wizard**. But if the **Add-in** subcommand of the **Tools** menu is activated, a number of add-ins can be selected, of which **Analysis ToolPak** should be checked. This will result in extending the **Tools** menu with the command **Data Analysis**. After this item has been selected, a number of choices is given (not all appear immediately on the screen), from which **Histogram** should be chosen. The control menu given in Panel 14.3 then appears.

The input range must be entered either via the keyboard or using the mouse. The same is true for the bin range. Input and bin ranges may contain descriptive labels which are ignored. If the bin range is omitted, the system makes up its own bin range by selecting a number of equal ranges between the minimum and the maximum of the

Panel 14.3 The Histogram Menu

input range. If the output is to be entered on the same sheet, the North-West corner of the output range should be indicated.

The spreadsheet then calculates the frequency distribution (the name histogram actually refers to the associated column chart) and puts it in the range G1:H13, see Panel 14.2.

The Histogram menu indicates that the results may also be put in a new worksheet or a new workbook. An alternative histogram, cumulative percentages, and a graphical result are also possible.

The frequencies in the range H2:H13 do not have a live link to the input range. The output range gives the frequencies of the input range when the command was executed.

14.1.3 The Frequency Function

An alternative to the Histogram command is the function FREQUENCY which provides a live link, so that, if the values in the input range or bin range change, this will be reflected in the results. This is illustrated in Panel 14.4.

The frequency function has two arguments: FREQUENCY(*input range, bin range*).

FREQUENCY is an *array function*, which means that the result is not a single cell but an array or range. Each cell of the output range displays the same formula. Such an array function is entered in a special way, described in the following steps:

Panel 14.4 Frequency Distribution Using Frequency Function

	A	B	C	D	E	F	G	H
1	No.	Customer	Loca	Satisfactior		Bin Range		Freq.
2	1	Macleod	SW	91.4%		0%		0
3	3	Varsity	NE	86.4%		10%		0
4	4	LowCost	NE	75.1%		20%		0
5	6	Southridge	OT	70.9%		30%		0
6	7	Restorator	SE	70.5%		40%		1
7	9	Apple	SW	70.3%		50%		0
8	12	Alpine	SW	69.5%		60%		3
9	13	Precision	OT	69.5%		70%		8
10	15	Ronaks	NW	69.2%		80%		4
11	16	Universal	SE	68.3%		90%		1
12	19	Phoenix	SW	65.5%		100%		1
13	20	Horton	SW	63.4%				
14	21	Shaw	NW	62.7%				18
15	24	Stampede	OT	60.1%				
16	25	Elite	SE	55.9%				
17	27	Espinola	OT	54.3%				
18	28	Cosmos	SW	50.8%				
19	29	Felix	SE	30.4%				

1. Select the output range, in this case H2:H13.
2. Enter the function
   =FREQUENCY(D2:D19,F2:F12)
   Note that D2:D19 is the Input Range and F2:F12 is the bin range.
3. Enter the command
   Windows: CONTROL+SHIFT+RETURN
   Macintosh: COMMAND+SHIFT+RETURN.

The result is the array H2:H13 in which all cells have the above formula within curly brackets. Note that the link with the cells in the input range and the bin range is now live.

The range containing an array function can only be altered or deleted as a whole. To delete it, the entire range should be selected.

Once the frequencies are known, it is useful to calculate the corresponding relative frequencies, which is done in column I in Panel 14.5. Cell H14 contains the sum of the frequencies, SUM(H2:H12) which is used for the range I2:I12, with as formula for I2, =H2/$H$14.

Frequencies can also be used to obtain cumulative relative frequencies. In column J the percentage of customers is calculated that obtain at most the percentage indicated in the bin range of column F, with J2 having as formula =I1+H2. More

Panel 14.5 Relative and Cumulative Frequencies

	F	G	H	I	J	K
1	Bin Range		Freq.	Rel. Fr.	C.Fr.Up	C.Fr.Dn
2	0%		0	0%	0%	100%
3	10%		0	0%	0%	100%
4	20%		0	0%	0%	100%
5	30%		0	0%	0%	100%
6	40%		1	6%	6%	100%
7	50%		0	0%	6%	94%
8	60%		3	17%	22%	94%
9	70%		8	44%	67%	78%
10	80%		4	22%	89%	33%
11	90%		1	6%	94%	11%
12	100%		1	6%	100%	6%
13						
14			18	100%		

interesting is the number of customers having more than a certain percentage, which is given by column K. Cell K12 has as formula =K11+I12, which is copied upwards. The numbers in column K are to be interpreted as the percentages of customers having more than the satisfaction percentages in the column F, one row higher. Hence 78% of customers have a percentage grade of more than 60%.

14.2 Rank and Percentrank

The customers may be ranked according to satisfaction, as is illustrated in Panel 14.6. This can be done by entering 1 into cell E2, selecting the range E2:E19, and invoking the command **Edit, Fill, Series**. The same is done by the function

RANK(*number, range*),

where *number* is the number cell to be ranked and *range* the range of the numbers among which it is to be ranked. An optional third nonzero argument allows ranking in ascending order. Cell E2 is therefore given the formula

=RANK(D2, D$2:D$19),

which is copied downwards.

Use of the RANK function has the advantage that it is independent of the order of the data. For a large database, sorting may not be desirable. Furthermore, the RANK function is live in the sense that it reflects changes in the data.

The rank of a number may also be expressed in terms of percentages, with the highest observation 100%, the lowest, 0%, and the rest spaced in between. The result is called *percentrank*. This quantity can be calculated by a simple transformation of the rank, giving F2 the formula

$$=(E\$19-E2+1)/E\$19$$

which can be copied downwards.

Alternatively, the function

=PERCENTRANK(range, number)

can be used, so that F2 is given the formula

=PERCENTRANK(D$2:D$19,D2)

which is copied to F2:F19.

Note that this formula is also independent of the order of the data. If the outcomes of the function PERCENTRANK and the simple formula are compared, they are not precisely the same. The reason for this is not clear.

Panel 14.6 Rank and Percentrank

	A	B	C	D	E	F	G
1	No.	Customer	Loc.	Satisf.	Rank	Percentrank	
2	1	Macleod	SW	91.4%	1	100%	
3	3	Varsity	NE	86.4%	2	94%	
4	4	LowCost	NE	75.1%	3	88%	
5	6	Southridge	OT	70.9%	4	82%	
6	7	Restorator	SE	70.5%	5	76%	
7	9	Apple	SW	70.3%	6	71%	
8	12	Alpine	SW	69.5%	7	65%	
9	13	Precision	OT	69.5%	8	59%	
10	15	Ronaks	NW	69.2%	9	53%	
11	16	Universal	SE	68.3%	10	47%	
12	19	Phoenix	SW	65.5%	11	41%	
13	20	Horton	SW	63.4%	12	35%	
14	21	Shaw	NW	62.7%	13	29%	
15	24	Stampede	OT	60.1%	14	24%	
16	25	Elite	SE	55.9%	15	18%	
17	27	Espinola	OT	54.3%	16	12%	
18	28	Cosmos	SW	50.8%	17	6%	
19	29	Felix	SE	30.4%	18	0%	

14.3 The Median, Quartiles, and Percentiles

What satisfaction did the customer in the middle have? The middle observation is called the *median*. Since there are an even number of customers, there is no middle observation, but it can be estimated by taking the average satisfaction of customers ranked 9 and 10, which is 68.7%.

Alternatively, the function

MEDIAN(*range*) =MEDIAN(D$2:D$19),

may be used, which gives the same result.

The concept of the median may be extended to that of quartiles, deciles, and percentiles. The first quartile is, in principle, the observation separating the first 25%

and the remainder, the second quartile is the median, and the third quartile is a value separating the first 75% and the remainder. This is the basis of the QUARTILE function, which is defined as:

QUARTILE(*range, quart*).

Panel 14.7 illustrates the use of this function. Cell I2 contains the formula

=QUARTILE(D$2:D$19, H2)

which is copied to I2:I6.

The first quartile (quart = 1) is the observation at 25% of the customers ranked from low to high, which is customer 0.25*18 = 4.5, that is in between Shaw and Stampede, so that the average is taken, which is about 61%. The second quartile is the same as the median, and the third quartile should be the average of Southridge and Restorator. The 0-th quartile should be the satisfaction at the bottom of the scale, but since this is not defined, the system estimates this to be the lowest number, 30.4%. The fourth quartile is explained in the same way.

Deciles are defined in terms of 10%, while percentiles are based on general percentages. The function percentile is similar to quartile and is defined as follows:

PERCENTILE(*range,percent*)

The lower right-hand part of Panel 14.7 illustrates its use. Cell I9 contains the formula =PERCENTILE(D$2:D$19,H9), which is copied downwards. The results obviously involve interpolations.

Panel 14.7 Quartiles and Deciles

	A	B	C	D	E	F	G	H	I
1	No.	Customer	Loc.	Satisf.	Rank	Percentrank		Quart	Quartile
2	1	Macleod	SW	91.4%	1	100%		0	30.4%
3	3	Varsity	NE	86.4%	2	94%		1	60.8%
4	4	LowCost	NE	75.1%	3	88%		2	68.7%
5	6	Southridge	OT	70.9%	4	82%		3	70.4%
6	7	Restorator	SE	70.5%	5	76%		4	91.4%
7	9	Apple	SW	70.3%	6	71%			
8	12	Alpine	SW	69.5%	7	65%		%	Decile
9	13	Precision	OT	69.5%	8	59%		0%	30.4%
10	15	Ronaks	NW	69.2%	9	53%		10%	53.3%
11	16	Universal	SE	68.3%	10	47%		20%	57.6%
12	19	Phoenix	SW	65.5%	11	41%		30%	62.8%
13	20	Horton	SW	63.4%	12	35%		40%	65.1%
14	21	Shaw	NW	62.7%	13	29%		50%	68.7%
15	24	Stampede	OT	60.1%	14	24%		60%	69.5%
16	25	Elite	SE	55.9%	15	18%		70%	70.3%
17	27	Espinola	OT	54.3%	16	12%		80%	70.8%
18	28	Cosmos	SW	50.8%	17	6%		90%	78.5%
19	29	Felix	SE	30.4%	18	0%		100%	91.4%

14.4 Percentile Based Groups

Numerical results are often expressed in terms of categories indicated by a letter. For example, the best 10% of the results are said to belong to Class A, the next 20% to Class B, and so on. The problem is then to assign to each item, in this case to each customer, a class identification.

An example of this is found determining student letter grades from numerical grades, when so-called *grading on a curve* takes place. For example, the top 6% of students get an A, the next 8% an A–, the next 10% a B+, and so on, see Panel 14.8, which represents the so-called curve in a column chart, and the range G3:H13 in Panel 14.9.

Let us interpret the satisfaction of the customers in the previous example as the numerical marks of 18 students which should be converted into letter grades according to the given percentages. The data are given in column B which are used to obtain the percentage ranks in column C. These must be converted into letter grades such that 6% receive an A, 8% an A–, and so on.

Panel 14.8 Fixed Grade Distribution

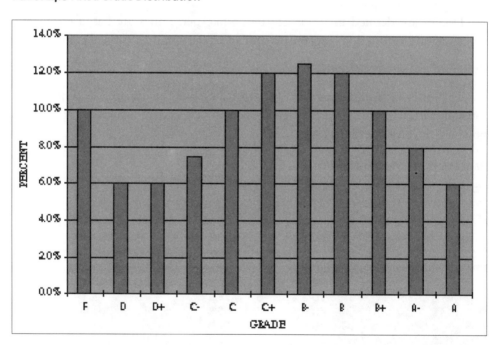

This is done by using a numerical lookup function. From the grade distribution in the range H3:H13, a cumulative grade distribution is built in the range H2:H13 by giving H2 a value of 0 and H3 the formula =H2+G3 which is copied downwards. Cell H13 is given a small positive perturbation (0.001 is added) to include 100% in the A class. After the letter grades are added in the range I3:I13, the range H2:I13 can be used as a lookup table for letter grades.

Cell D2 can now be given the formula

=VLOOKUP(C2,NLT,2)

where NLT is the name of the lookup table. Cell D2 is copied downwards, which leads to the required letter grades. The range A2:D19 may be sorted again with the column A as the primary key to obtain the original student records order.

Panel 14.9 Grading on a Curve

	A	B	C	D	E	F	G	H	I
1	Sl. No.	Perc.Gr.	Perc.Rank	L.Grade				NLT	
2	13	30%	0%	F		Grade	Percent	0%	F
3	7	51%	6%	F		F	10%	10%	D
4	9	54%	12%	D		D	6%	16%	D+
5	5	56%	18%	D+		D+	6%	22%	C-
6	15	60%	24%	C-		C-	8%	30%	C
7	3	63%	29%	C-		C	10%	40%	C+
8	16	63%	35%	C		C+	12%	52%	B-
9	14	66%	41%	C+		B-	12%	64%	B
10	11	68%	47%	C+		B	12%	76%	B+
11	12	69%	53%	B-		B+	10%	86%	A-
12	8	70%	59%	B-		A-	8%	94%	A
13	4	70%	65%	B		A	6%	100%	
14	1	70%	71%	B		Sum	100%		
15	18	70%	76%	B+					
16	2	71%	82%	B+					
17	10	75%	88%	A-					
18	6	86%	94%	A					
19	17	91%	100%	A					

14.5 Frequency Distributions for Labels

It is possible to obtain a label frequency distribution by first converting the labels to numbers by means of a lookup function, and then generating the frequency distribution of these numbers, as illustrated in Panel 14.10

The five locations are assigned numbers in the coding table F3:G7, which is given the name CT. This table is used in lookup functions in column D, where D2 has the formula:

=LOOKUP(C2,CT,2,0),

which is copied downwards.

The array frequency function is then constructed in the range H3:H7 by selecting this range, entering the function

=FREQUENCY(D2:D19,G3:G7),

and completing the array function by the special array code CONTROL (Macintosh: COMMAND) + SHIFT + RETURN.

In the next chapter an alternative method for obtaining a label frequency distribution is discussed.

Panel 14.10 Frequency Distribution for Location

	A	B	C	D	E	F	G	H
1	No.	Customer	Location	#		CT		
2	1	Macleod	SW	4		Loc.	Bin R.	Freq.
3	3	Varsity	NE	2		NW	1	2
4	4	LowCost	NE	2		NE	2	2
5	6	Southridge	OT	5		SE	3	4
6	7	Restorator	SE	3		SW	4	6
7	9	Apple	SW	4		OT	5	4
8	12	Alpine	SW	4				
9	13	Precision	OT	5				
10	15	Ronaks	NW	1				
11	16	Universal	SE	3				
12	19	Phoenix	SW	4				
13	20	Horton	SW	4				
14	21	Shaw	NW	1				
15	24	Stampede	OT	5				
16	25	Elite	SE	3				
17	27	Espinola	OT	5				
18	28	Cosmos	SW	4				
19	29	Felix	SE	3				

Exercises

14.1. After sorting customers according to location, find the number in each location with the COUNT function.

14.2. How can bin range intervals be obtained that include the lower bound instead of the upper bound?

14.3. Apply the RANK function to a range containing labels. What is the result? Do the same with PERCENTRANK.

14.4. Find out the difference between the outcomes of the PERCENTRANK function and the direct formula based on rank.

14.5. Classify the customers of the example into four equal groups, to be indicated as Satisfied, OK, Fair, and Unsatisfied, using a numerical lookup table.

Assignment

14.1 The Student Record Case II

Given is the sheet C1DATA on the accompanying disk with class records for 100 students.

(a) Determine the average over all assignments for each student, and make a frequency distribution of these averages.

(b) Make a graph of the numerical averages and the year of first registration determined by the first two digits of the student ID number. Is there a relationship?

(c) Determine the average of assignment percentages for MGMT, SS, SC, and GEN students.

(d) Using a lookup function, determine the letter grades corresponding to the numerical averages for each student.

(e) Make a frequency distribution, using the Histogram command, of the numerical grades with a bin range corresponding to the letter grades.

(f) Do the same as in Question 5 by means of the FREQUENCY function.

(g) Determine using the FREQUENCY function, the number of students in the faculties MGMT, SS, SC, and GEN.

Chapter 15
Statistical Functions for Databases

This chapter discusses more advanced database features using as an example an oil and gas production company reviewing its gas holdings. First the data for gas production and the application of elementary statistical functions to these data are presented. Then it is shown how database statistical functions can be used to obtain information about selected subsets of the data. It is shown how a label frequency distribution can be obtained by a combination of a database statistical function and the Data, Table command. Following this, it is explained how a similar combination is used to obtain tables comparing wells in different locations. Finally, yet another combination is used to obtain the supply curve for natural gas for this company.

In this chapter you will learn the following spreadsheet commands and functions:

- AVERAGE(*range*)
- MIN(*range*)
- MAX(*range*)
- COUNT(*range*)
- VAR(*range*)
- STD(*range*)
- VARP(*range*)
- STDP(*range*)
- COUNTIF(*range, criteria*)
- SUMIF(*range*)
- DSUM(*database, field, criteria*)
- DAVERAGE(*range*)
- DMIN(*range*)
- DMAX(*range*)
- DCOUNT(*range*)
- DVARP(*range*)
- DSTDP(*range*).

15.1 Gas Holdings and Statistical Functions
Consider an oil and gas production company that wants to review its gas holdings. The company has interests in 15 gas wells, the data for which are reproduced in Panel 15.1. The data given are well number, province, production capacity (in m^3 per day), fixed costs (in \$ per year), variable costs (per m^3 produced), and working interest (ownership percentage).

The annual revenue can be calculated as follows. If it is assumed that the entire production capacity is used, the annual production for Well number 1 is 693*365 m^3.

Panel 15.1 Gas Holdings Data

	A	B	C	D	E	F	G
1	DB					Price	$1.00
2	Well#	Prov.	Pr.C.	F Costs	V.Costs	W.I.	Ann.Rev.
3	1	Alb	693	$76,200	$0.86	92%	($37,525)
4	2	Alb	9838	$157,800	$0.55	29%	$422,847
5	3	B.C.	4203	$190,600	$0.37	64%	$496,563
6	4	Alb	6937	$295,000	$0.38	79%	$1,007,126
7	5	Sask	409	$37,800	$0.86	89%	($15,041)
8	6	B.C.	394	$37,800	$0.72	64%	$1,579
9	7	Alb	3736	$113,400	$0.59	97%	$432,322
10	8	Alb	592	$50,600	$0.85	81%	($14,732)
11	9	Alb	759	$37,800	$0.71	32%	$13,613
12	10	Sask	860	$25,000	$0.42	84%	$131,932
13	11	B.C.	6812	$235,000	$0.76	34%	$122,989
14	12	B.C.	6851	$140,600	$0.46	22%	$266,141
15	13	Alb	797	$76,200	$0.45	38%	$31,843
16	14	Sask	1416	$50,600	$0.39	68%	$179,977
17	15	Alb	1586	$63,400	$0.43	65%	$173,269

The revenue per m^3 is the price, $1.00, minus the variable costs. Revenue per well is then equal to revenue per m^3 times annual production minus fixed costs. This should be multiplied by the working interest. The formula for G3 is therefore:

=(C3*365*(PRICE-E3)-D3)*F3

where PRICE is the name of cell G1.

Spreadsheets have a number of statistical functions, some of which, SUM(*range*), COUNTA(*range*), and COUNT(*range*), have already been introduced. Panel 15.2 gives a statistical summary of the gas holdings database, which uses these functions as well as a number of other ones. The other functions are AVERAGE(*range*), which gives the average of the numeric cells in the range, MIN(*range*) and MAX(*range*), giving the minimum and the maximum of these cells, and VAR(*range*) and STDEV(*range*), which calculate the variance and the standard deviation of the numeric cells. The two last functions refer to the sample variant of both functions, which means that division is made by $n-1$, the number in the sample, so that the variance estimate is unbiased. The functions VARP and STDEVP calculate the variance and standard deviation based on the population, so that division by n takes place.

In Panel 15.2 the range E20:E26 contains these functions written as labels for the annual revenues of the 15 gas holdings, and D20:D26 gives the resulting values. If the maximum and the minimum of a set of numbers are known, the range, defined as the difference between the two, is easily found, as in cell D27, which has as formula =D23–D22.

Panel 15.2 Statistical Summary Gas Holdings Data

	A	B	C	D	E	F	G
19	Statistical Summary						
20	Sum			$3,212,902	=SUM(G3:G17)		
21	Average			$214,193	=AVERAGE(G3:G17)		
22	Minimum			($37,525)	=MIN(G3:G17)		
23	Maximum			$1,007,126	=MAX(G3:G17)		
24	Number of wells			15	=COUNTA(G3:G17)		
25	Variance			7.9088E+10	=VAR(G3:G17)		
26	Standard Deviation			$281,225	=STDEV(G3:G17)		
27	Range			$1,044,651	=D23-D22		

In the following section the use of database statistical functions will be described, which enable the calculation of statistical measures for subsets of the data based on criteria ranges. Two functions are available for a simple selection based on just one column. These are the functions COUNTIF and SUMIF.

Suppose the number of wells in Alberta is required. This would be given by the function

=COUNTIF(B3:B17,"Alb"),

where the first argument is the range of the provinces column (see column B in Panel 15.1), and the second the criteria.

The sum of the production of all wells with a production higher than 1,000 would be given by the function

=SUMIF(C3:C17,>1000).

For these two functions, the criteria are limited to those applying to the data range selected, so that the production of all wells in Alberta cannot be determined with this sum function.

15.2 Database Statistical Functions

Suppose that the sum of annual revenues from all wells in Alberta must be found. This can be done by sorting or filtering all records and then using the function SUM for the annual revenues of the Alberta wells which are now adjacent. The disadvantage of this approach is that the entire database, which may be quite large, must be changed to obtain this result. *Database statistical functions* make it possible to obtain results from a subset of records that can be precisely indicated.

To enable a more precise identification, the data should be organized in a database consisting of a range of rows and columns, as for example the range A2:G17 which is named DB in Panel 15.1. The first row contains the column headings or *field names* and the remaining rows the records.

Panel 15.3 Use of Database Statistical Functions

	A	B	C	D	E	F	G
29	CRIT1						
30	Prov.						
31	Alb						
32							
33	Statistical Summary for Alberta Wells						
34	Sum			$2,028,762	=DSUM(DB,7,CRIT1)		
35	Average			$253,595	=DAVG(DB,7,CRIT1)		
36	Minimum			($37,525)	=DMIN(DB,7,CRIT1)		
37	Maximum			$1,007,126	=DMAX(DB,7,CRIT1)		
38	Number of wells			8	=DCOUNTA(DB,7,CRIT1)		
39	Variance			1.2834E+11	=DVAR(DB,7,CRIT1)		
40	Standard Deviation			$358,243	=DSTDEV(DB,7,CRIT1)		
41	Range			$1,044,651	=D37-D36		

To indicate the desired data, a *criteria range* is used, which is in this case A30:A31, see Panel 15.3. It consists of the field name 'Prov.' and below it the label for the desired data, 'Alb'. The field name in A20 should be precisely the same as that in the first row of the database range DB. To ensure this, it is best to copy it with the **Copy** command.

As the criteria range is probably used a number of times, it is convenient to name it. In Panel 15.3 the name CRIT1 was chosen. Note: The name CR1 cannot be used, as this is the name of the cell in column CR and row 1.

The sum of annual revenues of wells in Alberta can now be found by the formula in cell G34:

=DSUM(DB,7,CRIT1),

where DB and CRIT1 are the names of the database range and the criteria range. The second argument, here 7, is the number of the column or field in the database over which the sum should be taken.

Instead of a label criterion such as province, a numerical criterion may be used. Suppose the sum of annual revenues of all wells with a positive annual revenue should be found. This is done by creating another criteria range CRIT2 in the range A44:A45, copying the field name Ann.Rev. to the A44, and >0 in A45, see Panel 15.4. The range A 33:G37 is then copied to a range with an upper right-hand cell A47, and the formulas in the database functions are modified by replacing CRIT1 by CRIT2.

It is also possible to have combinations of criteria. If two criteria must both be satisfied at the same time, this is called the logical AND combination, and if of two criteria at least one must be satisfied, this is called the logical OR combination.

Suppose the sum of annual revenues of all Alberta wells with a positive annual revenue should be found. This is the AND combination of the two criteria. The criteria range should now contain two columns with field names Prov. and Ann. Rev. and the two cells containing the criteria in the next row, see the range A19:B20 in Panel 15.5.

Panel 15.4 A Numerical Criterion

	A	B	C	D	E	F	G
43	CRIT2						
44	Ann.Rev.						
45	>0						
46							
47	Statistical Summary Wells with Positive Revenues						
48	Sum			$3,280,200	=DSUM(DB,7,CRIT2)		
49	Average			$273,350	=DAVERAGE(DB,7,CRIT2)		
50	Minimum			$1,579	=DMIN(DB,7,CRIT2)		
51	Maximum			$1,007,126	=DMAX(DB,7,CRIT2)		
52	Number of wells			12	=DCOUNTA(DB,7,CRIT2)		
53	Variance			8.1538E+10	=DVAR(DB,7,CRIT2)		
54	Standard Deviation			$285,548	=DSTDEV(DB,7,CRIT2)		
55	Range			$1,005,547	=D51-D50		

Panel 15.5 Criterion Ranges for AND and OR Combinations

	A	B
19	Prov.	Ann.Rev.
20	Alb	>0
21		
22	Prov.	Ann.Rev.
23	Alb	
24		>0

On the other hand, criteria that need not be satisfied at the same time should be entered in different rows of the criteria range, as indicated in the A22:B24, which selects data that concern wells in Alberta or wells with a positive revenue. Criterion ranges obviously allow the selection of complex combinations of data that may be of use in many situations.

15.3 Label Frequency Distribution

Database statistical functions may be used in conjunction with Data Tables to generate frequency distributions for labels or to perform sensitivity analysis with respect to prices or any other parameter. This section deals with label frequency distributions.

Let us find the frequency distribution of gas wells according to province. For this, the function DCOUNT will be used, which needs a criteria range. As such, the range A28:A29, named CRIT2, see Panel 15.6, will be used, which contains the heading 'Prov.' and the label 'Alb'.

Panel 15.6 Frequency Distribution of Wells According to Province by Data Table

	A	B	C	D	E	F
28	Prov.		8	=DCOUNT(DB,2,CRIT2)		
29	Alb	Alb	8	{=TABLE(,A29)}		
30		B.C.	4	{=TABLE(,A29)}		
31		Sask	3	{=TABLE(,A29)}		

Consider now the formula entered in C28 and displayed in D28,

=DCOUNT(DB,2,CRIT2),

which shows up as 8, as there are 8 Alberta gas wells in the database. This is the key cell in an application of Data Table with a table range of B28:C31. The labels for the three provinces are entered into the index range of the table, B29:B31. As input cell A29 is used. Data Table will take first the label Alb in B29, put it into A29, calculate the value of C28, and assign it to C29, and so on.

This can also be applied to find the frequency distribution of letter grades in the course database. Consider the first three columns of Panel 15.7. The letter grades in C2:C6 should be counted in a DCOUNT function. The range C2:C6 contains lookup functions which result in the displayed letter grades.

Panel 15.7 Frequency Distribution of Letter Grades

	A	B	C	D	E	F	G
1		%	L.Gr.	L.Gr.		1	=DCOUNT(DB,3,CRIT)
2	Aalhus	76%	B	C	F	0	{=TABLE(,D2)}
3	Abbott	88%	A-		D	0	{=TABLE(,D2)}
4	Adam	83%	B+		D+	0	{=TABLE(,D2)}
5	Adler	61%	C		C-	0	{=TABLE(,D2)}
6	Aziz	84%	B+		C	1	{=TABLE(,D2)}
7	NLT				C+	0	{=TABLE(,D2)}
8	0%	F			B-	0	{=TABLE(,D2)}
9	45%	D			B	1	{=TABLE(,D2)}
10	50%	D+			B+	2	{=TABLE(,D2)}
11	55%	C-			A-	1	{=TABLE(,D2)}
12	60%	C			A	0	{=TABLE(,D2)}
13	65%	C+					
14	70%	B-					
15	75%	B					
16	80%	B+					
17	85%	A-					
18	90%	A					

A criteria range CRIT is created in D1:D2, which is used in the DCOUNT function in F1, the formula of which is displayed in G1. The result 1 is correct, as there is one C in C2:C6. F1 is a key cell of the table F1:G12 for Data Table. Cell D2 functions as input cell.

The result is displayed in G2:G12. All cells in this range form an array with the common formula {=TABLE(,D2)}.

15.4 A Comparison of Averages

A similar combination of database functions and Data Table may be used to compare the operations in the various provinces. Suppose that we are interested in comparing for the three provinces the number of wells, the averages of production capacity, fixed costs, variable costs, working interest and annual revenues, and also total annual revenue. For Alberta these are given by the following formulas entered in the range B24:H24 (see Panel 15.8):

=DCOUNT(DB,2,CRIT2)
=DAVERAGE(DB,3,CRIT2)
=DAVERAGE(DB,4,CRIT2)
=DAVERAGE(DB,5,CRIT2)
=DAVERAGE(DB,6,CRIT2)
=DAVERAGE(DB,7,CRIT2)
=DSUM(DB,7,CRIT2)

Panel 15.8 Data Table used for Comparison of Provinces

	A	B	C	D	E	F	G	H
20	Prov.							
21	Alb							
22								
23		No.W	Prod.Cap.	F. Costs	V. Costs	W.I.	An.R.Av.	An.R.T.
24		12	3682	$118,600	$0.52	56%	$273,350	$3,280,200
25	Alb	8	3117	$108,800	$0.60	64%	$253,595	$2,028,762
26	B.C.	4	4565	$151,000	$0.58	46%	$221,818	$887,272
27	Sask	3	895	$37,800	$0.56	80%	$98,956	$296,868

The criteria range CRIT2 is A20:A21. The cells in B24:H24 may now be used as key cells in an application of Data Table, with as table range A24:H27 and as column input cell A21. The index column A25:A27 should contain the names of the provinces. The format of the key cells will be copied to those below it. The results are given in the range B25:H27.

These results may be illustrated by graphs. For averages, such as that of annual revenues, column charts are appropriate, see Panel 15.9, whereas for totals, such as number of wells or total annual revenue, pie charts may be used, see Panel 15.10.

Panel 15.9 Column Chart for Average Revenues

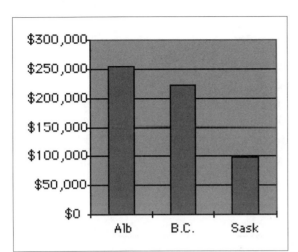

Panel 15.10 Pie Chart for Total Revenues

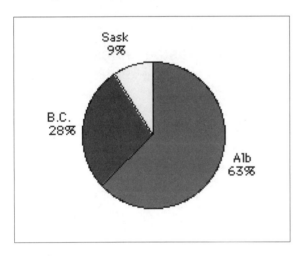

15.5 Derivation of the Gas Supply Curve

Of great interest in terms of economics is the impact of a price variation on the quantity of gas produced and the resulting revenues. If the net revenue of a well is negative, that well will be shut down and production will be zero. Since the net revenue depends on the price, it will have a direct impact on revenues but also an indirect one via the production quantity. It is therefore of interest to find out how the production quantity and the total revenue will depend on the price. This can be done by the Data Table command.

Total production for wells with a positive revenue is given by

=365*DSUM(DB,3,CRIT1),

where CRIT1 is the range A20:A21 (see Panel 15.11), which has in A21 the formula =G2>0. Total revenue is given by

=DSUM(DB,7,CRIT1).

These two formulas should be evaluated for varying prices, say for prices varying from 0.50 to 1.50 by 0.10. This can be done using Data Table.

Panel 15.11 gives the format and the final result. The table range is B23:D34. The variable to be varied is price and its values are given in B24:B34. The cells C23 and D23 contain the above formulas for production and revenues. As input cell B18, named PRICE, is used, which so far contained a price of $1.00. Data Table then generates the range C24:D24.

Panel 15.11 The Impact of Price on Production and Revenue

	A	B	C	D	E	F
18	Price	$1.00				
19						
20	Ann.Rev.					
21		0	(=G2>0)			
22			Production	Ann. Rev.		
23			16128985	$3,280,200	=DSUM(DB,7,CRIT1)	
24		$0.50	4896840	$16,982	{=TABLE(,B18)}	
25		$0.60	11567215	$451,856		
26		$0.70	12930855	$1,043,858		
27		$0.80	13221760	$1,742,365		
28		$0.90	15985175	$2,485,392		
29		$1.00	16128985	$3,280,200		
30	Price	$1.10	16345065	$4,085,403		
31		$1.20	16747295	$4,925,888		
32		$1.30	16747295	$5,782,381		
33		$1.40	16747295	$6,638,873		
34		$1.50	16747295	$7,495,366		

At a price of $0.50 production is nearly 5 million m^3 but revenue is only $16,982. A price increase to $0.60, a 20% increase, increases production by 140%, and the revenue is now $450,000. Above a price of $1.20, production does not increase any more, but, of course, revenues go up.

The relation between price and quantity produced represents, in economic terms, the supply curve. This company supply curve is given in Panel 15.12. It is almost perfectly elastic at prices of $0.50–$0.60, but that at prices around $1.00 it is inelastic, while above $1.20 it is perfectly inelastic. This is a short-run supply curve. In the long run more wells will be drilled if the price is high enough, which will result in higher production, so that the curve will not be perfectly inelastic at high prices.

The second column of the table gives net revenues for varying prices. Panel 15.13 gives this relationship in a column chart. Revenues go up linearly with the price. For prices above $1.20 this is understandable, because the quantity produced does not change anymore. For lower prices it is the combined effect of increased quantities and an increased profit margin, which results in approximately the same revenue increase per unit price increase.

Panel 15.12 Company Supply Curve for Gas

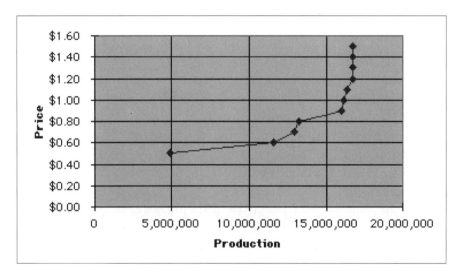

Panel 15.13 Annual Revenue for Varying Prices

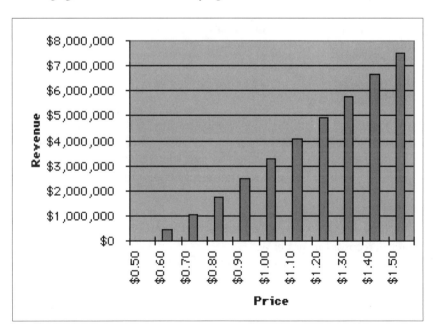

Exercises

15.1 How do statistical function react to blank cells and cells with labels in their ranges?

15.2 Find the annual productive capacity of all wells that are either in Alberta or Saskatchewan that have at least a working interest of 50%.

15.3 Using Data Table, make a frequency distribution of the annual revenues for the three provinces.

Assignments

15.1 Real Estate Database

On the accompanying disk is the file C1DATA containing information about 100 properties listed for sale.

(a) Copy the records of the 10 properties with the highest price. Do the same for the 10 most recently listed, for the 10 oldest in terms of year built, and the 10 largest in terms of ft^2.

(b) Make a frequency distribution in terms of the list prices and graph these in a chart named FIG1.

(c) Real estate commissions are 7% of the first $100,000 of the price, 6% of the amount over this up to a price of $200,000, and 5% of the amount over $200,000. Using a lookup function, determine for each property the sales commission. Graph for all properties sales commissions against list price, and name the chart FIG2.

(d) (i) Using database statistical functions, find the number of properties in the N.W., their average size, their average year built, and their average list price.

(ii) Using Data Table, do this for all locations.

(iii) Same as in (b) but now for properties with a listing price under $200,000.

(e) (i) Assuming that all houses listed are the same, construct a supply curve for houses, naming it FIG3.

(ii) Assuming that each house supplies living space given by its ft^2, construct a supply curve for living space, naming it FIG4.

15.2 The Car Sales Database Case

Given is the file C2DATA containing information about 100 cars listed for sale.

(a) Extract all records for model W.

(b) Make a frequency distribution of the list prices and graph these in a chart named FIG1.

(c) The prices for new models have been given in A3:B7. Using a lookup function, determine for each listing the new-price and the listing price as a percentage of the new price. Graph the list prices against the new-prices in a chart named FIG2.

(d) (i) Using database statistical functions, find the number of cars of model W, their average kilometres driven, their average year built, and their average list price.

   (ii) Using Data Table, determine for each model and each year the average list price. (The table will contain cells with ERR when the database statistical function finds no applicable cells.)

   (iii) Same as in (b) but now for cars with with less than 40,000 km on the odometer.

(e) (i) Assuming that all cars are the same, construct a supply curve for cars, naming it FIG3.

   (ii) Suppose a car buyer is able to resell any of these cars at a price of $7,500 and must offer each of the 100 sellers the same price (the buyer is a nondiscriminating monopsonist). To maximize profits, what price would be selected? Illustrate with a chart named FIG4.

Chapter 16
Investment Portfolio Evaluation

This chapter deals with the periodic evaluation of an investment portfolio in terms of internal rate of return. After an initial section on date and time functions, the determination of the internal rate of return for non-integral time periods is developed. If initial holdings and transactions throughout the period are given, the final holdings may be determined using database functions and the Data Table command. Once the final holdings are known, the return of the portfolio can be found.

In this chapter you will learn the following spreadsheet commands and functions:

- Format Cells Date
- DATE(*Year,Month,Day*)
- NOW()
- RATE(*nper,PV,FV*)

16.1 Date and Time Functions

Any organization of activities requires a measurement of time. Many different time measuring units exist, the most important of which are years, quarters, months, weeks, days, hours, minutes, and seconds. The conversion from one time measurement unit into another one is straightforward and uses universally known constants, but always requires at least one multiplication or division.

Another important feature of time measurement is the choice of origin. Western society dates years from the birth of Christ, Islamic societies use the year of the Hegira (flight of Mohammed from Mekka to Medina, 622 A.D.), whereas in Japan the initial year of the reigning emperor is chosen.

The spreadsheet has taken as its point of origin January 1, 1900, and as its unit of time measurement, days. Any date it represents as the number of days since January 1, 1900. The conversion into the usual representations of dates and time are done, rather ingeniously, via formatting, so that the number remains the same, but its display changes. This means that the number 0 can be displayed as 00-Jan-00. The date format can be chosen as a submenu of the command **Format**, **Cells**, **Date** after which a number of choices of date representations are presented.

If the number is 36,000, one of the formats converts it into 24-Jul-98, while another format represents it as 7/24/98. Somewhat inconsistently, the control bar gives the formatted date, not the underlying number.

The **Format**, **Cells**, **Date** command expresses values in one of the conventional time representations. A number of functions are available to do the reverse, converting conventional date formats into the spreadsheet value representations (which may then be formatted as dates). The function

=DATE(*year*,*month*,*day*)

can be used to enter a particular date. For example, DATE(98,1,1) gives the value representing that date, 35,796, which, formatted as a date, is displayed as 01-Jan-98. The function NOW() gives the current date, if the built-in clock of the computer has been set correctly.

The date functions may be used to calculate the number of days between two dates. For example, the number of dates between September 1, 1995 and January 1, 1999 is:

=DATE(99,1,1)–DATE(95,9,1)

which is 1,218.

16.2 Investment Evaluation for Non-Integral Periods

In the project evaluation discussed before, annual cash flows were considered. Receipts and payouts were implicitly assumed to take place at the same time of the year. In most cases this is a reasonable approximation of cash flows that will occur throughout the year, but in other cases a more precise evaluation is necessary. Consider the cash flows for a $10,000 bond with an annual interest rate of 10.4%. The bond was bought on January 27, Year 0 and sold on January 3 of the next year, see Panel 16.1. Three quarterly interest payments were received at the indicated dates.

Panel 16.1 Cash Flows for a $10,000 Bond

	A	B	C	D	E
1	Date	Cashflow			
2	27-Jan-00	($10,520)			
3	14-Apr-00	$260			
4	19-Jul-00	$260			
5	19-Oct-00	$260			
6	03-Jan-01	$10,450			
7	Sum	$710			
8					
9	Internal Rate of Return	7.01%	=(1+IRR(B2:B6,0.1))^4-1		
10	Using RATE	7.22%	=RATE((A6-A2)/365,,B2,SUM(B3:B6))		

One way to deal with this is to divide the year into quarters, and assume that the cash flows occur at the same time in each of these quarters, and then use the IRR function to find the return per quarter via

=IRR(B2:B6,10%).

This quarterly return can be used to obtain the corresponding annual return by multiplication by 4, or more precisely by obtaining the compounded return, giving the complete formula

=(1+IRR(B2:B6,10%))^4−1

which results in 7.01%, see B9 in Panel 16.1. As the dates of purchase, January 27, Year 0 and that of selling, January 3, Year 1, differ by 24 days, this rate of return is not very accurate.

A higher precision can be obtained by using time units that are smaller than quarters, for example months. In this case two rows are inserted between each cash flow, representing the months in between . This leads to a much larger spreadsheet and, in this case, does not improve the accuracy.

A different approach is to assume that the interest payments are received at the same time as the sales revenue. In that case the internal rate of return is determined by the value of the initial investment (present value), the final value of the investment (future value) and the time elapsed between the two (term). The internal rate of return can then be calculated using the equation

$$FV = PV^*(1+r)^{\wedge}n$$

where FV stands for future value, PV for present value, n for the term, and r for the internal rate of return.

This equation can be solved for r, so that the internal rate of return is given by

$$(FV/PV)^{\wedge}(-n)-1.$$

The same formula is implemented in the spreadsheet by the function

=RATE(*nper,PV,FV*).

It has been entered in cell B10 of Panel 16.1 as

=RATE((A6−A2)/365,B2,SUM(B3:B6))

which results in 7.22%.

This approach can be made more accurate by taking instead of the three amounts of $260, their future value at January 3, 1997, using some given interest rate. This complicates matters again and requires some value for the interest rate.

A more satisfactory approach uses present value definitions applied to non-integral time measurement. The present value at time t_1 of an amount A to be received at time t_2 if the interest rate for discount purposes is r, is given by

$$A^*(1+r)^{\wedge}(-(t2-t1)) = A^*(1+r)^{\wedge}(t1-t2).$$

This is implemented in Panel 16.2. Cell C2 has the formula

=B2*(1+B$11)^((A$2−A2)/365)

Panel 16.2 Rate of Return With Present Values

	A	B	C	D	E
1	Date	Cashflow	Present Value		
2	27-Jan-96	($10,520)	($10,520)	=B2*(1+B$11)^(($A$2-A2)/365)	
3	14-Apr-96	$260	$256		
4	19-Jul-96	$260	$251		
5	19-Oct-96	$260	$247		
6	03-Jan-97	$10,450	$9,766		
7	Sum	$710	$0		
8					
9	Internal Rate of Return	7.01%	=(1+IRR(B2:B6,0.1))^4-1		
10	Using RATE	7.22%	=RATE((A6-A2)/365,,B2,SUM(B3:B6))		
11	IRR, Present Value=0	7.49%			

where B11 is the interest rate. This is copied to the range C3:C6. Cell C7 contains the sum and therefore the present value of the cash flow.

Since the internal rate of return is the rate of interest resulting in a present value of 0, it can be obtained by changing B11 until C7 is 0 or close to it. The command **Tools, Goal Seek** can be employed for this purpose. The result is 7.49%, substantially larger than the two previous estimates.

16.3 Final Holdings for Investment Portfolio

Usually a number of investment securities are held at the same time, which constitutes an investment portfolio. Spreadsheets can be used to keep record of holdings and transactions and to evaluate the periodic performance of a portfolio. To explain this, the data will be used of a small portfolio consisting of some bonds, shares, and mutual funds, see Panel 16.3.

The data consist of the portfolio holdings at the start of Year 0, the transactions during that year, and the cash income of the portfolio. It is assumed that the prices per January 1, Year 1, are also available, to be used later. Required are the portfolio holdings per January 1, Year 1, the present values and rates of return of the entire portfolio, of the bonds, mutual funds, and shares, and of the various securities during the year. The determination of the final holdings is treated in this section, and that of the present values and rates of return in the next one.

To obtain the portfolio holdings at the start of Year 1, the holdings at the beginning of Year 0 and the changes brought about by transactions must be combined. For a very small portfolio like this one this could be done entirely manually and visually, but for one that is only slightly larger, a more systematic approach is needed.

What is first needed is a list of securities that occur in the initial holdings or in the transactions, or in both, and the number of units held in these securities and their class after one year. This list can be made up by selecting the range A2:D16 and using the command **Data, Filter, Advanced Filter, Unique** to obtain the names and

Panel 16.3 Records for Investment Portfolio

	A	B	C	D	E	F
1	Initial Holdings					
2	Date	Security	Class	Units	Price	Value
3	02-Jan-00	BCGas	S	1200	$16.25	
4	02-Jan-00	Weldwood	S	800	$11.38	
5	02-Jan-00	Cda 10	B	9	$1,036.20	
6	02-Jan-00	Nova 10.75	B	5	$1,020.50	
7	02-Jan-00	AltInc	M	1263	$7.17	
8	02-Jan-00	BTInt	M	845	$7.31	
9	Transactions					
10	02-Feb-00	PWACorp	S	1000	$5.63	
11	18-Mar-00	BCGas	S	-600	$17.00	
12	26-Jun-00	Alta 9.75	B	5	$1,067.20	
13	05-Aug-00	TrimCan	M	500	$12.40	
14	24-Oct-00	BTInt	M	-845	$8.20	
15	29-Nov-00	Cda 10	B	3	$1,078.00	
16	Income					
17	06-Jan-00	Nova 10.75	B			$269
18	07-Jan-00	Cda 10	B			$450
19	07-Jul-00	Nova 10.75	B			$269
20	11-Jul-00	Cda 10	B			$450
21	12-Jul-00	Alta 9.75	B			$244

corresponding class without duplication. Note that the names of securities in the initial holdings and the transactions should be precisely the same to avoid duplication. This is copied to the range H3:I12 of Panel 16.4. The result is sorted alphabetically.

For any given security, say Alta 9.75, the number of units at the start of Year 1 can be found as the sum of the initial holdings for that security plus that of the number of units found in the transactions part (positive means that the security was bought, negative, that it was sold) in which there may be multiple transactions. This can be captured by a DSUM-function with as criteria range H13:H14:

=DSUM(DB,4,H13:H14)

which is entered in I15, resulting in a display of 5. The range DB is defined as A2:D16.

Cell I15 is used in a Data Table command. The arguments are the security names in H16:H24, which have been copied from H4:H12. With a table range of H15:I24, and an input cell of H15, the command results in the numbers in I16:I24.

The number of units of BTInt is 0, as all units have been sold, so that this security may be deleted in the final holdings. In a larger portfolio there may be a number of such securities, which makes their manual removal time-consuming. Securities with 0 units may be removed by the sorting according to the number of units column in descending order, after which the securities with 0 units at the bottom may be deleted. Sorting again according to the securities' names restores the previous order.

The securities with a nonzero number of units can now be copied to B23:B30, and the corresponding number of units are copied to D23:D30. The corresponding class can be found by using H4:I12 as a lookup table by giving C23 the formula

=VLOOKUP(B23,$H$4:$I$12,2)

which results in the label B. C23 is copied downwards to C23:C30.

Panel 16.4 Determination of Final Holdings

	A	B	C	D	E	F	H	I	J
1	Initial Holdings								
2	Date	Security	Class	Units	Price	Value	Security	Class	
3	02-Jan-00	BCGas	S	1200	$16.25				
4	02-Jan-00	Weldwood	S	800	$11.38		Alta 9.75	B	
5	02-Jan-00	Cda 10	B	9	$1,036.20		Alt Inc	M	
6	02-Jan-00	Nova 10.75	B	5	$1,020.50		BCGas	S	
7	02-Jan-00	Alt Inc	M	1263	$7.17		BTInt	M	
8	02-Jan-00	BTInt	M	845	$7.31		Cda 10	B	
9	Transactions						Nova 10.75	B	
10	02-Feb-00	PWACorp	S	1000	$5.63		PWACorp	S	
11	18-Mar-00	BCGas	S	-600	$17.00		Trim Can	M	
12	26-Jun-00	Alta 9.75	B	5	$1,067.20		Weldwood	S	
13	05-Aug-00	Trim Can	M	500	$12.40		Security		
14	24-Oct-00	BTInt	M	-845	$8.20		Alta 9.75	=DSUM(DB,4,H13:H14)	
15	29-Nov-00	Cda 10	B	3	$1,078.00			5	
16	Income						Alta 9.75	5	
17	06-Jan-00	Nova 10.75	B			$269	Alt Inc	1263	
18	07-Jan-00	Cda 10	B			$450	BCGas	600	
19	07-Jul-00	Nova 10.75	B			$269	BTInt	0	
20	11-Jul-00	Cda 10	B			$450	Cda 10	12	
21	12-Jul-00	Alta 9.75	B			$244	Nova 10.75	5	
22	Final Holdings						PWACorp	1000	
23	01-Jan-01	Alta 9.75	B	5			Trim Can	500	
24	01-Jan-01	Alt Inc	M	1263			Weldwood	800	
25	01-Jan-01	BCGas	S	600			{=TABLE(,H14)}		
26	01-Jan-01	Cda 10	B	12					
27	01-Jan-01	Nova 10.75	B	5					
28	01-Jan-01	PWACorp	S	1000					
29	01-Jan-01	Trim Can	M	500					
30	01-Jan-01	Weldwood	S	800					

16.4 Evaluation of the Investment Portfolio

After the final holdings of the portfolio have been determined, the portfolio can now be evaluated. First the prices per January 1 of Year 1 for the securities in the final holdings must be entered. This can best be done at this stage and not earlier, as at an earlier stage it is not known which securities will be in the final holdings. Panel 16.5 contains these prices in the range E23:E30.

The evaluation of the portfolio for the year takes place under the assumption that the securities of the initial holdings are bought at the prices at the start of the year, and the securities in the final holdings are sold at the prices at the end of the year. The value in F3 therefore contains the formula =–D3*E3 which is copied to the range F3:F8, and that in F23, =D27*E27, which is copied to F23:F30. Buying a security means that the corresponding sum must be paid, so that cell F10 has as content =–D10*E10, which is copied to F10:F15. This completes all the values in column F. Cell F31 contains the sum $4,467, which indicates the net revenue of the portfolio during the year. But we are also interested in the present value and the internal rate of return of the entire portfolio and of its parts. Note that the NPV and IRR functions cannot be used on the range F3:F30, as successive rows do not represent equidistant time intervals.

For each value in column F the corresponding present value at the start of the year must be determined. First an interest rate for discount purposes is entered, say 10% in B33, which is given the range name INT. Cell G3 is then given the formula,

$$=F3*(1+INT)^{((\$A\$3-A3)/365)},$$

which is copied to the range G3:G30, after which the content of G9, G16, and G22 is erased. F31 is now copied to G31, which displays then the present value of the portfolio at 10%, which is –$1,250. B34 is made equal to G31.

The corresponding internal rate of return can be found by varying the interest rate until the present value is approximately equal to 0, which happens for an interest rate of 7.62%. The command **Tools, Goal Seek** may be used for this purpose.

To find the present value and internal rate of return for a class of securities, the DSUM function must be used, see the range A36:C37 in Panel 16.5. First the name INT is given to B36, which will contain the discount interest rate, say 10%. The criteria range is C36:C37. Let us define A2:G30 as the database range DBALL. The formula for the present value in B37 is then

$$=DSUM(DBALL,7,C36:C37),$$

which equals –$1,728. By varying B36 until B37 is approximately 0, the corresponding internal rate of return is found, which happens to be 0.49%.

The present value and internal rate of return for a security, say BCGas, are found in a similar way, see A39:B40 in Panel 16.5.

The present value of all classes or of all securities can be found by means of the Data Table command. Let us do this for an interest rate of 7.62%, which is the internal rate of return for the entire portfolio, so that the present values must sum to 0. Let E33:E34 be the criteria range for the database function in G34

$$=DSUM(DBALL,7,E33:E34).$$

F33 is called INT, the Data Table range is F34:G43, and the input cell is E34.

The result of the command is given in G34:G43. This indicates that BCGas was by far the worst investment. This can be made more clear by first sorting the present values according to decreasing size, which results in an arrangement as in I35:J43. Panel 16.6 gives the resulting bar graph.

Panel 16.5 Portfolio Evaluation

	A	B	C	D	E	F	G	H	I	J
1	Initial Holdings									
2	Date	Security	Class	Units	Price	Value	Pr. Value			
3	01-Jan-00	BCGas	S	1200	$16.25	($19,500)	($19,500)			
4	01-Jan-00	Weldwood	S	800	$11.38	($9,100)	($9,100)			
5	01-Jan-00	Cda 1D	B	9	$1,036.20	($9,326)	($9,326)			
6	01-Jan-00	Nova 10.75	B	5	$1,020.50	($5,103)	($5,103)			
7	01-Jan-00	AltInc	M	1263	$7.17	($9,056)	($9,056)			
8	01-Jan-00	BTInt	M	845	$7.31	($6,177)	($6,177)			
9	Transactions									
10	01-Feb-00	PWACorp	S	1000	$5.03	($5,025)	($5,590)			
11	18-Mar-00	BCGas	S	-600	$17.00	$10,200	$10,043			
12	26-Jun-00	Alta 9.75	B	5	$1,067.20	($5,336)	($5,149)			
13	05-Aug-00	TrimCan	M	500	$12.40	($6,200)	($5,935)			
14	24-Oct-00	BTInt	M	-845	$8.20	$6,929	$6,527			
15	29-Nov-00	Cda 1D	B	3	$1,078.00	($3,234)	($3,024)			
16	Income									
17	06-Jan-00	Nova 10.75	B			$269	$269			
18	06-Jan-00	Cda 1D	B			$450	$450			
19	07-Jul-00	Nova 10.75	B			$269	$259			
20	11-Jul-00	Cda 1D	B			$450	$433			
21	12-Jul-00	Alta 9.75	B			$244	$235			
22	Final Holdings									
23	01-Jan-01	Alta 9.75	B	5	$1,090.00	$5,450	$5,083			
24	01-Jan-01	AltInc	M	1263	$7.85	$9,915	$9,210			
25	01-Jan-01	BCGas	S	600	$14.25	$8,550	$7,943			
26	01-Jan-01	Cda 10	B	12	$1,095.00	$13,140	$12,207			
27	01-Jan-01	Nova 10.75	B	5	$1,067.50	$5,338	$4,958			
28	01-Jan-01	PWACorp	S	1000	$6.00	$6,000	$5,574			
29	01-Jan-01	TrimCan	M	500	$12.64	$6,320	$5,871			
30	01-Jan-01	Weldwood	S	800	$12.00	$9,600	$8,918			
31	Total					$4,467	($0)			
32										
33	Int. R. of R.	7.65%			Security	7.62%				
34	Present Value	($0)			Alta 9.75		$	148		
35						Alta 9.75	$	148	Cda 10	$741
36	Int. R. of R.	0.49%	Class			AltInc	$	155	Nova 10.75	$384
37	Present Value	($0)	S			BCGas	$	(1,514)	BTInt	$351
38						BTInt	$	350	AltInc	$157
39	Int. R. of R.	-6.59%	Security			Cda 10	$	739	Alta 9.75	$148
40	Present Value	($0)	BCGas			Nova 10.75	$	383	PWACorp	($15)
41						PWACorp	$	(16)	TrimCan	($64)
42						TrimCan	$	(64)	Weldwood	($180)
43						Weldwood	$	(182)	BCGas	($1,511)

Panel 16.6 Present Values of Securities

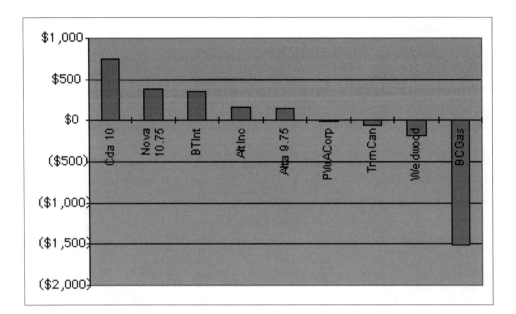

Exercises

16.1 Assume that the investment portfolio of section 16.3 also contains stock dividends, which means that at certain times the number of units of a security is increased by a certain percentage. How can this be incorporated into the spreadsheet and the rate of return calculations?

16.2 Assume that commissions are charged when securities are bought and sold. It is assumed that for the transactions given commissions are already included in the cash flows, but not in the prices and values of the holdings per January 1, 1993. The mutual funds can be redeemed without any charge, but security sales with a total amount less than $5,000 are charged a commission of 2.5% and higher amounts, 1.5%. Take this into account in the rate of return calculations.

Assignments

16.1 Credit Balance

A company wants to analyze its sales invoices and the corresponding payments it receives. Both can be found on the accompanying disk in the file C1DATA with the invoices having positive values and the payments negative ones. Use the same file to answer the following questions.

(a) Extract the data for the sales invoices.

(b) Make a frequency distribution of the values of these invoices with limits 0–<200, 200–<500, 500–<1000, 1000–<2000, 2000–<3000, 3000–<4000, >4000.

(c) Using database statistical functions, find the number of invoices, the average value per invoice, and the total value of sales invoices , for clients A, B, C, and D.

(d) The company is considering giving discounts to each client based on the total value of sales invoices for each client. The discount would be for values between $5,000 and $10,000: 2.5% of the value above $5,000; for values between $10,000 and $20,000: $125 plus 5% of the value above $10,000;, and for values above $20,000: $625 + 7.5% of the value above $20,000. Create a lookup table for this discount, and use it to find out what the discount would be for A, B, C, and D, and determine by what percentage it would decrease the total sales value for 1988.

(e) Turning back to the original database, find for each of the dates the balance of unpaid invoices, and use this and the dates to find the capital costs of the unpaid balances over 1988, assuming that the daily interest (with daily compounding) is 0.05%.

(f) Find the average unpaid balance over all the dates, and use this for an alternative estimate of the annual capital costs, assuming that the annual interest percentage is 20%. Is this average unpaid balance the same as the average for the entire year? Explain.

index

Index